Teaching Fluency
Beyond the
Primary Grades

Midge Madden
and Jane Sullivan

■SCHOLASTIC

New York • Toronto • London • Auckland • Sydney
Mexico City • New Delhi • Hong Kong • Buenos Aires

Dedications

To my mother, Harriet Ernst, and my grandfather, Eddy Cuenod. They took my hand and led me to
wondrous worlds unlocked only through reading.
—M.M.

To Nathaniel Hatch who taught me much about patience and perseverance. Thank you for helping
me write those lessons.
—J.S.

Acknowledgements

To write and see hard-fought words appear in a published book is reward enough for many authors. But
for those who know the power of collaboration, there exists a different sense of celebration. As co-authors we
remember countless hours writing and revising, eagerly read early morning and late night e-mails, continued
words of support and encouragement … and finally, a book! Yes, that is indeed cause for celebration.

But we will miss those times, so first, we must acknowledge this special friendship that bonds us as authors.
And we know a new book yet to be born awaits us. We feel it!

We would be remiss if we did not thank all of the teachers, parents, and students whose voices brought our
book to life. Thank you to an amazing teacher, Kathy Carhart and her fifth grade students at the William
Winchester Elementary School in Westminster, Maryland.

Thank you to David Jackson and his wonderful group of fifth graders at Upper Township Elementary
School in Upper Township, New Jersey. And thank you to Norfa Hernandez, Guatemalan teacher extraordinaire,
and her reading students at Escuela Integrada in Antigua, Guatemala. Thanks as well to the students whose
names appear throughout the pages of the lessons and to their parents who generously allowed us to use their
children's work.

And thank you to our dear friend, Janice Betts whose grandchildren speak so knowingly about tests and
fluency assessment.

Most of all, thanks to Nathaniel and Joey and their grandmother, Cathy, for their willingness to let Jane
"try out" fluency lessons!

Finally, we owe the beauty of the finished manuscript to our editor, Sarah Longhi. Thank you for many
hours of diligent reading and excellent suggestions to make our writing better. Your enthusiasm and encouragement moved us to finish a book we're proud to share with others.

Edited by Sarah Longhi
Copyedited by Erich Strom

Cover design by Brian LaRossa
Cover photo: © Banana Stock/Jupiter Images
Interior design by Melinda Belter
ISBN-13 978-0-439-90016-4
ISBN-10 0-439-90016-6

Contents

Introduction

"Close your eyes and feel the poem. Try to let the words and music wash over you as you experience the poem," Kathy urges her fifth graders.

"Okay, Mrs. Carhart, but c'mon, we want to hear the song!" pleads Peter.

PORTRAIT OF A CLASSROOM WHERE FLUENCY MATTERS

Kathy smiles, hand poised above the CD player. "Be sure you're ready. The title is 'Concrete Angel.'" She pushes the play button.

Twenty-seven fifth graders make not a sound. Heads down, eyes closed, they seem mesmerized as they each struggle to interpret the narrative poem set to music.

After the last note is sung, Kathy softly challenges the class, "What do you think happens? How did you feel as you listened? Take five minutes to freewrite your interpretation and feelings." She moves around the classroom as the children scribble ideas. When they've finished, she directs, "Now we'll do a text rendering. As we go around the circle, I want each of you to read only what you have written."

"It's so-o-o-o sad," reads Destinee. "Did she have to die? She just wants to be loved . . ."

Peter tears up as he reads his words. "I really feel this, Mrs. Carhart. It's just unfair . . . and cruel."

Each child reads. Then, silence. Kathy distributes the text of "Concrete Angel" and says, "Now, listen again but read the words of the song. Feel free to sing along quietly if you wish." Several do sing softly, and as the last note dies, they clamor, "Play it again, Mrs. Carhart. We want to sing it together."

And this class of fifth graders read-sings, voices together, narrating a poignant text with emotion and empathy.

"Beautiful!" Kathy and I catch each other's eyes. "That's how we want you to read your own poems! Anyone want to try?"

Peter's hand shoots up. Kathy nods and he stands. "My poem is about street life," begins Peter, "and I hope you feel the pain as much as I do." He slowly walks to the front of the room, closes his eyes, and sighs. Then he stares intently at his classmates and performs his poem.

Street Life
I stare out the window, some days it's cold, some days hot,
Everyday there is someone out there
on the street.
I wonder how they survive,
the hobos, as my mom calls them.
But observing, I learn how they think, how they act,
and what I never want to be.
Drunks, as my father calls them.

At the Door
Today I'm at the door, pondering.
They probably think fighting off dogs is a living,
But some days like today they die—
too much alcohol my teacher says,
Too much alcohol.

Light
The streets are terrible,
Claiming lives here and there.

Death
Some alleys are dark, some alleys are light,
All alleys are gloomy.
Gloom within gloom, never to see the light of day.

The Smell
One day it came,
Rolling through town thick like a fog,
Burning,
Driving all other smells away like
ants assaulting air fresheners.
It came from the harbor.
The fresh smell of alcohol.

Peter dramatically repeats the last line, then asks, "Do you get it? You know, the evils of alcohol?"

"Oh, yeah," says Sarah. "We get it. And it's really good."

"Can I read mine, now, Dr. M?" Zach asks. I nod and smile. And another eager reader begins.

Writers, readers, *and* performers. This group of fifth graders has learned well not only the importance of words but the power of oral reading performances. In Kathy's class, students find reasons to read and write. They discover that others listen to their words when they're well crafted and well read. Students in Kathy Carhart's class know that fluency does indeed matter.

But how did these students get here? What does Kathy do that inspires her students to want to perform texts? As you might guess, turning older students into eager, fluent readers does not happen overnight; yet exciting possibilities exist if we're willing to make fluency instruction part of our lessons. Kathy's poetry reading shows that when we give students authentic and meaningful opportunities to engage in expressive speaking and oral reading, they work to improve the sound and expression of their reading. Furthermore, they see the importance of these tasks in their social and academic lives. This book is built on the premise that targeted, student-centered, and age-appropriate practices for teaching fluency are needed to reach today's middle school students.

Fluency has become one of the hottest topics in literacy today (Cassidy & Cassidy, 2005). With the No Child Left Behind Act having identified fluency as one of the five components of effective literacy teaching, we teachers are faced with greater curriculums that demand more explicit fluency instruction. We recognize fluent readers when we hear them—dramatic, expressive voices of CNN news commentators or well-rehearsed student performances during Readers Theater. And we know when fluency is missing—struggling voices giving disjointed, inaccurate readings. But how do we *teach* students to read fluently, particularly older, struggling readers? How do we move these students from hesitant, word-by-word readers to confident speakers of texts?

These questions frame the underlying purpose of our book: to look at effective ways to teach fluency to older readers. We share our successful teaching experiences with fifth- and sixth-grade fluent and nonfluent readers. We've designed activities that appeal to all readers, since all students have difficulties with fluency, albeit with different levels of texts. Peter, for example, in Kathy Carhart's class, is an excellent reader who shows a strong command of language. Yet he still needed to practice his phrasing and emphasis to perform his poem well. Likewise, struggling readers in Kathy's class also learned to perform their poems. Alex often needs extra help understanding texts and writing with focus and detail. But when a subject captures his interest, he works to achieve what comes more easily to his peers. And he, like Peter, learns the importance and power of fluent reading. During his turn to share his poem, classmates listen intently as Alex reads:

Martin Arrested
Happy day
Maryland, 1855
An ordinary day
Chased through a grassy field
Great day for hide and seek
Jail
Racism
Blacks can't play with whites
Martin finds out
Police come
Take Martin away
Away to jail, violently
Meets Cody, a new friend
Cody is black, Martin is black

Free
Another Martin
Martin Luther King, Jr.
Making a speech
I have a dream speech
Martin and Cody . . .
Free
More peace
More Friends
"Come live with me"
Martin asks
Cody nods "yes"
Maryland 1863
Blacks can play with whites
Good friends Alex, Zack, Cody, Martin
Let's go home.

Although his poem may not be as coherent as Peter's, Alex, nonetheless, took a chance at expressing his own ideas in his own voice to his peers and succeeded in reading smoothly, expressively, and with emotion.

We believe that students at all levels gain fluency when lessons inspire them to *want* to read well. So, in this book, we describe lessons in which students write, learn new vocabulary, become articulate speakers, and interpret texts. These lessons teach more than fluency. They engage the students in activities that promote strong literacy skills—with fluency as a major focus and final result.

How This Book Is Organized

Each chapter begins with a portrait of students engaged in a lesson on developing fluency. These students are usually in a fifth- or sixth-grade classroom, interacting with the teacher or one of the authors. The portraits place the reader in the kind of classroom setting where good literacy teaching happens. They may focus on an introduction to a lesson, a snapshot of students practicing a strategy, or a final project.

Chapter 1 presents an overview of fluency. We define and discuss the components of fluency and provide various examples of students who read fluently. Our purpose is to help you gain a deeper understanding of fluency and the needs of older readers, needs that subsequent chapters address through portraits and lesson presentations.

Chapters 2 through 4 each focus on a different aspect of fluency instruction. The classroom portrait introduces the chapter's fluency skill. Following the portrait is a detailed description of the skill and a series of sample lessons that we have used with fifth- and sixth-grade students. We also suggest texts that are particularly appropriate for older students and offer ways to adapt the lessons for younger or older students.

Chapter 5 includes strategies and resources for assessing fluency and determining how to best support your readers. We close with an epilogue that shows how fluent, engaged reading can open exciting opportunities for self-expression in our students' lives.

CHAPTER ONE

What Do Educators Mean by *Fluency?*

Watching waves roll toward the beach at the shore is one of life's pleasures. There is a rhythm to the movement—steady, even, predictable. Language, too, has a rhythm that is steady, even, predictable. We choose to call this rhythm *fluency.*

Fluency Defined

Pikulski and Chard (2005) suggest the following definition of *fluency* as applied to reading:

> Reading fluency refers to efficient, effective word-recognition skills that permit a reader to construct the meaning of text. Fluency is manifested in accurate, rapid, expressive oral reading and is applied during and makes possible, silent reading comprehension.

We agree. Fluency is not a simple trait of language; it's a complex skill. And mastering it is equally complex. Our students become fluent readers when they've mastered the components of fluency. But what are these components? We believe they are word recognition, automaticity, correct phrasing, and prosody, or expressive reading. We listen for these components in the voices of our students as they read aloud.

For example, when Jane's 11-year-old nephew, Nate, reads a new text, he hesitates on every third or fourth word, relying solely on the decoding skills he's learned. He does not recognize the words "at sight" or, as we say, automatically. The result is a slow, halting reading that lacks correct phrasing and expression. In direct contrast, when Jane's student Rebecca reads aloud, the words flow smoothly. Same age. Same grade. The difference? Rebecca recognizes each word without even thinking about it, while Nate has to decode many of the words. Rebecca reads with automaticity. Nate needs to build his sight vocabulary to develop that automaticity. When Rebecca reads aloud, it sounds like she is talking. She groups words into logical phrases with brief pauses between the phrases. She pauses at punctuation marks. Her voice goes up when she reads a question. She sounds excited when the sentence ends in an exclamation point. In other words, her oral reading reflects the prosody or natural expression that we expect in fluent reading. All of these traits—word recognition, automaticity, correct phrasing, and prosody —are what we listen for when we judge the fluency of our students' reading: the "accurate, rapid, expressive oral reading" of which Pikulski writes.

DEEP VS. SURFACE STRUCTURE OF FLUENCY

Pikulski (2006) urges us to consider whether we should treat the skill of fluency superficially (i.e., teach simple lessons in reading faster) or emphasize the deeper construct (i.e., teach students to develop the automaticity, correct phrasing, and prosody required for smooth, expressive reading)—so that students can *understand* what they are reading.

As authors, we have chosen the path Pikulski recommends—to focus on that deeper construct. We are not interested in teaching our students simply to "read faster"; for us, fast reading is *not* synonymous with fluent reading. We want students to read with understanding. And that requires *all* the components that make up this thing we call fluency. Some of the lessons in this book, such as vocabulary development (Chapter 3), focus on a specific component of fluency. Others, such as Readers Theater (Chapter 2), require a combination of the components that lead to the ultimate outcome—smooth reading, no unintentional hesitations, and the phrasing and natural expression we hear when we speak. This kind of fluency, so closely aligned with meaning-making, becomes for us the deep construct or structure that we support. We urge teachers to choose this construct as well and reject the notion that rapid reading alone is an accurate measure of fluency.

The Effect of Fluency on Comprehension

In discussing the relationship between fluency and comprehension, Pikulski tells us that "efficient, effective word-recognition skills" will "permit a reader to construct meaning of text" (2006). The choice of the word *permit* is noteworthy. There is no guarantee that readers who demonstrate "accurate, rapid, and expressive reading" grasp the full meaning of the text. Comprehension is more complex than fluency and depends upon the connections readers make between the text and what they already know. Jane recalls a moment years ago when she asked one of her fifth-grade students to read a section of their textbook aloud—cold, without having seen it previously. The young girl stood and read the paragraph with a fluency that pleased Jane. The boy sitting next to her raised his hand. "Can Diane tell us what she read?" he asked. Jane nodded to the girl. "Go ahead, Diane." A puzzled expression crossed Diane's face. She didn't know! She had concentrated on the sound of her voice rather than on meaning.

Diane's performance shows us that smooth oral reading does not necessarily indicate comprehension. So, when our lessons focus on teaching fluency, we provide opportunities for students to practice reading aloud with the expression and rhythm that characterizes fluency. But we also make sure that they're connecting with the text and can truly grasp the meaning.

In the following chapters, we include sample lessons that we have used or observed in classrooms, lessons designed to help students improve their reading fluency. We have chosen the middle grades as our focus because we believe that fluency instruction remains critical for students as they progress through school. As text difficulty increases, so also does the need for fluency and comprehension, so the lessons in fluency we create for our older readers look very different from those designed for beginning readers. In books for beginning readers, authors usually use the vocabulary and language structures that children commonly hear and/or use themselves. But writing for older readers incorporates descriptive words and phrases like "the water detonated" or "the bells rang me out of my reverie." Not many students, even sophisticated speakers, use such language in their conversations. Additionally, the syntax becomes more formal. Long, complex sentences send fifth and sixth graders struggling through a maze of words, unable to apply the phrasing or prosody they used so well with more familiar sentence structures.

Thus, when texts contain unfamiliar phrases and complicated syntax structures, achieving fluency is a challenge for older readers. Comprehension is a crucial element of fluent reading—and vice versa. For this reason, our lessons provide both fluency and comprehension practice. Finally, effective fluency lessons must capture the students' interest. For us, fluency instruction becomes more effective when students *choose* to hone their oral reading skills and we strive to create opportunities for our middle-grade students to experience fully the benefits of learning to be fluent readers.

Factors That Determine Fluency

FACTOR 1:
AUTOMATICITY OF WORD RECOGNITION

A student's fluency with text written at one level does not guarantee fluency with unfamiliar texts at a higher level. For example, we can expect students with a sight vocabulary of 500 words to read a text consisting of words solely from that list with little or no hesitation. But texts with more sophisticated words cause that same student to pause, stumble, and lose the rhythm. The level of automatic word recognition impacts the reader's fluency. In other words, a reader's ability to read fluently depends on the difficulty of the text.

Because many words in English are spelled regularly, we teach students to use phonics skills when they meet unfamiliar words. This is a practical approach that provides young readers with a certain amount of independence. There is the danger, however, that older readers will continue to depend upon decoding strategies rather than commit the whole word to their sight-words memory bank. We argue that phonics, syllabication, accenting—practices so useful when first meeting an unknown word in print—should over time become secondary to automatic recognition. Unless readers increase sight-word knowledge, they cannot develop the automaticity that fluency requires. Fluency then permits a reader to attend to meaning. But, as we pointed out earlier, older students often encounter words in their reading whose *meaning* is unknown. So it becomes critical to teach middle- and upper-grade students to focus not only on automatic recognition of words but on meanings as well.

FACTOR 2:
APPROPRIATE PHRASING

The fluent reader needs to be able to group words into meaningful phrases, which requires familiarity with the syntax the writer uses. Punctuation gives the reader some clues. An exclamation point, a question mark, or a period at the end of a sentence, a colon or dash, a comma—all these seemingly inconsequential marks contribute to the intended expression and meaning. Each demands a different interpretation. The meaning of the words *I want an apple* changes based on the end punctuation. Place a period at the end (*I want an apple.*) and you have a simple statement. A question mark suggests doubt or surprise (*I want an apple?*) while an exclamation mark (*I want an apple!*) indicates insistence.

Authors sometimes omit punctuation for purposes of style. As readers, we need to be alert to those games and solve the puzzles they raise. Jane tells of her confusion with a sentence that appeared in *Paula* by Isabel Allende. It read: *We left in a basket the letters.* Jane read and reread those simple words, trying to make sense of them: "*We left—in a basket the letters?* No. *We left—in a basket—the letters* . . . Ridiculous! Aha! *We left in a basket—the letters.*" Allende might have added commas to indicate where to pause. Or she might have rearranged the words to read: *We left the letters in a basket.* But she didn't. So Jane had to struggle for comprehension by playing with phrasing until she understood the author's intended meaning. Students need to learn this skill, too—which is why we have included a lesson on phrasing in the search for meaning.

Additionally, as the level of difficulty of texts increases, the written language structure tends to become more formal and more complicated than that of spoken language. A fifth-grade text, for example, tends to have longer, more complex sentences than a third-grade text. Authors of texts for older students often combine words in unfamiliar ways for stylistic effect. In *Walk Two Moons,* for example, Sharon Creech writes: *Days turned into months, months into years.* These are clearly delineated phrases but with a somewhat unusual syntax. When readers come to a sequence of words with phrasing that is new to them, their fluency suffers. When Nate, Jane's nephew, first read Creech's words, he missed the comma and thought the second *months* was a misprint. But, after a second reading, he said, "Oh! I get it now." And he reestablished fluency.

FACTOR 3:
PROSODY

A third factor that affects fluency is the natural expression that readers put onto their reading. We call this prosody. In the lesson we include on reading jokes aloud, Jane's two nephews, Nate and Joey, surprise her with the expression they use. *You* becomes *Ya* as in "Ya know whut"; *had to* becomes *hadda* and *wants to know* becomes *wanstano.* In familiar words and phrases, Nate and Joey slip easily into a slang that constitutes their ordinary speech—with a fluency that tells us they are interpreting the text correctly. Clear articulation of the written word is eclipsed by their natural speaking and inflection.

Nate and Joey prepare their joke script (Chapter 2, Lesson 2).

The Role of Reading Aloud

Many teachers today question the benefits of the "round-robin" technique of oral reading. Jane was surprised to discover this in her college reading class. She had called on a student to read aloud a short passage from the textbook and then describe the feelings she had experienced during the reading. The student stumbled through the unfamiliar text, misreading words, cheeks flushed and eyes downcast. It was clearly a painful experience. Jane has since abandoned the practice. Many teachers argue that oral reading, round-robin-style, helps students who will not or cannot read the selection on their own. But even when students can get through short sections of a passage without too much trouble, another dynamic often occurs. As one student reads aloud, the others are counting ahead to find the paragraph that will fall to them on their turn—and practicing the words so they will not stumble when called on. If these students are not listening to the text their classmates are reading aloud, and consequently missing critical information, how then can they put the ideas together to reach comprehension?

In *Good-Bye Round Robin* (1998), Opitz and Rasinski list eight possible problems that may result from round-robin reading:

- It provides students with an inaccurate view of reading.

- It can potentially cause faulty reading habits instead of effective reading strategies.

- It can cause unnecessary subvocalization.

- It can cause inattentive behaviors.

- It can work against all students developing to their full potential.

- It consumes valuable classroom time that could be spent on other meaningful activities.

- It can be a source of anxiety and embarrassment for students.

- It can hamper listening comprehension. (pp. 6–8)

Unfortunately, by discrediting round-robin-reading, we have inadvertently encouraged teachers to abandon oral reading completely. Many have switched to the practice of having students read silently and answer questions on what they read. But, the assumption that students will automatically build sight vocabulary and read silently with expression is, at best, a questionable one and certainly not one we can *hear* proof of. Listening to a student read aloud allows us to monitor fluency. Consequently, oral reading must be a part of our literacy instruction. In the oral reading lessons we include in this book, we demonstrate effective ways of guiding students to read orally.

In *The Fluent Reader* (2003), Rasinski points out that while fostering fluency, oral reading can also build confidence, create community, connect reading and writing, and strengthen decoding skills—but only when it is done right. The lessons on fluency in this book support these goals and they produce results: Each classroom snapshot clearly shows the manifold power of oral reading.

A proverb reminds us "a picture is worth a thousand words." We teachers can show our students a portrait of fluency when we read aloud to them. In David Jackson's classroom, where Jane currently spends most of her volunteer time, she waits eagerly for the signal that it is read-aloud time. David invites his students to bring their snacks and get comfortable on the carpet where his rocking chair sits. He brings the book that he is currently reading aloud, and settling into the chair and opening the book, he begins to read. As his first words fill the room, his students, proficient as they are in reading, prepare themselves for what they know will be an enjoyable 30 minutes. David models fluency, proper phrasing, reading with expression, and pausing at critical points. From time to time, he stops and shares thoughts of his own or invites a student to offer an opinion or an interpretation. The listeners get into the story with him, hanging on his every word. In a lesson we include in this book, Jane asks these students to figure out what makes a fluent reader. They know, not because someone has told them, but because every day their teacher *shows* them a fluent reader. And that picture is worth more than a thousand words.

Our students need to understand what we expect of them when we say "read fluently." They need to know what constitutes this fluency we prize so highly. And then, they need to improve their fluency—and their comprehension—through practice. In the chapters that follow, we first establish that our students understand what those skills are. Then we provide the instruction, and practice, that builds each of these skills so that, by putting the pieces together, our students become more fluent readers, orally and silently.

CHAPTER TWO

Techniques for Building Prosody

Visiting relatives in Seattle, I find myself with the opportunity to use my expertise as a reading specialist. My nephew Nate has been labeled a struggling learner and I have offered to assess his reading skills. So here we are, Nate and

Aunt Jane, looking for a quiet spot to work together.

PORTRAIT OF A STUDENT WHO DISCOVERS FLUENCY

"In here," I say, peeking into the small room that houses the TV. "It's empty for a change." The two of us settle back onto the couch and I lay the three books I've brought with me on the table in front of us. I turn to my companion. "We're here to work," I say. "Let's get started."

Nate glances at the cover of the first book. "I can't read that, ya know," he says confidently. Just as confidently, I reply, "We'll see." It turns out Nate knows himself better than I do. We look at the cover illustration and the title and author—*Miss Nelson is Missing* by James Marshall—talk about these features and then turn to the first page.

"Try reading this aloud for me," I say. Nate starts—he reads, "The kids in Room 207 were." And stops. The next word, *misbehaving*, stumps him. He makes a few unsuccessful attempts, I give him the word and he moves on to the next word "a-a-a-gai . . . n . . . again," he sounds out.

The session continues pretty much the same way—reading two or three words, then an attempt at decoding or using the context, sometimes successful, sometimes not. After a few minutes of this, I put the book aside and reach for an easier one. Same result. It doesn't take me long to pinpoint Nate's problem. He could write a book on phonics rules but has an extremely limited sight vocabulary for an 8-year-old.

What to do? I still have his attention. He doesn't act bored and chats about the illustrations. This is a smart kid, but one who's having trouble pulling the parts together to read with fluency. I want to end our session on an upbeat note so I pull out Margaret Wise Brown's *The Runaway Bunny*. The text is supported by illustrations, and with dialogue on each page and many repeating phrases, it's perfect for an impromptu Readers Theater.

"I love this book," I tell Nate. "Want to read it together?" He's agreeable, so off we go. I read the first two lines; Nate reads the next two. I help him with the troublesome words. He catches on to the repeating phrases quickly and really gets into it, hamming up his lines with gusto. We read the book again, this time switching roles. Nate's older brother, Joey, passes by and we call him in for our audience. We capture Grandma and perform again for her. Nate is really enjoying the attention. More important, as he reads and rereads, his phrasing improves, the hesitation disappears, and he reads with expression. Nate has demonstrated to me and to his family that when automaticity takes over, fluency kicks in.

Just as young children learn to speak with expression by imitating the oral language that surrounds them, so too do students learn fluent reading most easily by example. Children who are fortunate enough to hear adults read stories aloud intuitively apply that same prosody as they read the short sentences they encounter in their beginning reading books. But, as text becomes more difficult—as the sentences grow in length and unfamiliar words appear more frequently—some of our

Students reading scripts they've adapted from a novel (Lesson 3).

students revert to that word-by-word, nonexpressive reading that we teachers hear more than we would like. As in the example of Nate, with repeated practice, the fluent reading we look for in our students reappears. The key to success hinges on the difficulty of the text. They must be able to identify most words (at least 95 percent). They need to listen to good examples of fluent reading. And they also need the opportunity to practice—getting the words, the phrasing, the expression right. The lessons in this chapter demonstrate techniques we have used to give students those examples of fluent reading, and the coaching and opportunities to practice that will allow them to imitate those examples.

LESSONS IN THIS CHAPTER

Lesson One:
How Do We Recognize Fluency? (page 20)
Objective: Pinpoint the characteristics of fluent reading by analyzing fluent and nonfluent examples.

Lesson Two:
Reading Sentences Fluently (page 26)
Objective: Build sight vocabulary and practice phrasing and expression with joke scripts.

Lesson Three:
Using Readers Theater as a Method for Developing Fluency (page 33)
Objective: Evaluate fluency characteristics in Readers Theater performances of short, student-created scripts.

Lesson 1

How Do We Recognize Fluency?

TAUGHT BY JANE SULLIVAN IN DAVID JACKSON'S FIFTH-GRADE CLASS
UPPER TOWNSHIP ELEMENTARY SCHOOL, UPPER TOWNSHIP, N.J.

INTRODUCTION

People recognize fluency easily enough when they hear it. However, to help our students read fluently, they need to be able to pinpoint its characteristics. One way to do that is to have them analyze examples of fluent and nonfluent reading. What does the nonfluent reader do wrong? What does the fluent reader do right? In this lesson, the teacher guides students in a discussion about the characteristics that differentiate fluent from nonfluent reading. For the fluent reading example, we used an excerpt from a CD recording of Sharon Creech's *Replay*. And then we taped Jane, who taught the lesson, imitating a nonfluent reader reading a short excerpt from Beth Evangelista's *Gifted*. In that way, we could include multiple instances of characteristic errors of nonfluent reading. We also avoided using a struggling reader as a bad example.

Jane read as a nonfluent reader might read: phrasing incorrectly, hesitating on words, repeating phrases, and generally reading without expression. The object of this lesson is for students to understand the components of fluency—even if they cannot use technical terms such as *automaticity* or *prosody*.

PREPARATION AND MATERIALS

- Two taped examples of a 100-word excerpt at the expected reading level: one that illustrates nonfluent reading and one that illustrates fluent reading. (There are many CDs of popular children's books available for the example of fluent reading.) The taped example of nonfluent reading should illustrate errors nonfluent readers typically make.

- Copies of the sample texts for each student

- Clipboards, pencils (if students are away from their desks)

PROCEDURE, PURPOSE, AND NARRATIVE

1 STEP ONE

Introduce the purpose of the lesson: to recognize a "fluent reader."

Purpose

While students may be able to recognize "good oral reading," they may not have discovered on their own what the individual requirements are for fluency in reading. Here we give them an opportunity to identify the characteristics of fluent reading.

Narrative

David Jackson's students sit together on the carpet, waiting for the lesson to begin. "Today," I begin, "I want to talk a bit about fluent reading. I'm going to ask you to tell me how you know if someone is reading fluently or not. What exactly is he or she doing, or not doing? Okay?" Hands go up. "I know what fluency is," Sara offers. I signal her to save her comments for later and continue. ◆

2 STEP TWO

Hand out copies of sample texts. Students will be writing their comments on the back of that paper, so they will need pencils and a notebook or clipboard to lean on. Introduce the passage and play the tape with the example of nonfluent reading: slow hesitant reading, word errors, poor phrasing, ignoring punctuation, lack of expression. Have students follow along silently and identify what "the reader is doing wrong."

Purpose

It is easier to identify the components of fluency when you begin with an example of nonfluent reading, and then contrast it with one that is well done.

Narrative

I ask a few students to distribute the copies of the sample texts. "Look at that first paragraph on your page," I say. "It is from a book titled *Gifted* by Beth Evangelista. Did you all find it? Now, I'm going to play a tape of someone reading that paragraph. I want you to read along silently and focus on what the reader is doing wrong. Afterward, I will ask you about that." We listen to the tape. Some children giggle at the slow, halting reading. Most sit silently, obviously in pain for the reader. Most seem not to know that it is my voice they are listening to. ◆

3 STEP THREE

Give students an opportunity to analyze the kind of errors the reader made. First, allow them to brainstorm with a partner. Then, ask them to write down the examples they heard.

Purpose

Allowing students to discover the characteristics in pairs encourages shared learning.

Narrative

I turn off the tape. "I'd like you to turn to your partner and share with him or her what you heard that the reader did wrong. What made her reading nonfluent?" A buzz fills the classroom as the discussion continues for several minutes. I call time and ask them "Write on the back of your papers the errors you discussed." ◆

4 STEP FOUR

Review and discuss the students' analysis of the reading.

Purpose

Comparing notes with the group encourages learning.

Narrative

I ask for volunteers to tell the group what they discovered. Jessica raises her hand. "She stopped between words." "Why did she do that, do you think?" I ask. "She didn't know how to pronounce them?" guesses Jessica. I ask for a consensus: "Were there a lot of words she didn't know?" Heads nod all around.

"She should have done the five-finger challenge," says Brittany. "And what's that?" I ask. Brittany is ready with the answer. "You open the book to a page and look down it. Put up a finger for every word you don't know. Like this." She raises her hand with three fingers extended. "If you put up five fingers," she continues, "the book is too hard for you." I agree. "Very nice explanation, Brittany. Okay, are you ready for a new word?" I ask. A chorus of "yeahs" surrounds me.

"Here it is: *Automaticity*." I write the word on the chart paper and say, "To be a fluent reader, you need to know almost all of the words in the text you're reading automatically—without thinking, *What is that word?* That's one thing our reader couldn't do. What other mistakes did she make?"

Sara raises her hand. "She wasn't paying attention to the periods." "Okay," I agree. "Remember those times when we talked about periods and commas and question marks in your writing? They help your readers, help them understand what you're talking about. A fluent reader will pay attention to punctuation. Anything else?"

Rebecca raises her hand. "It was boring because she had no expression and she dragged out her words. She read everything the same. You didn't know if it was dialogue or just telling the story." Again, I nod in agreement. "By expression, do you mean the rhythm of the language? Loud or soft? Up or down? Excited or sad? Asking or telling?" I ask. Rebecca nods.

Evan adds to the discussion. "She didn't put the words together in the right way. She paused between words where she shouldn't have. Like *came poking in through* . . . she shouldn't have stopped there. She should have said *through my doorway.*" "Good example, Evan," I say. "We call that phrasing. She didn't phrase well; she didn't put the words together that belong together." ◆

5 STEP FIVE

Summarize the characteristics of fluent reading that students have identified.

Purpose
Providing actual examples of fluent and nonfluent reading helps students arrive at generalizations about the characteristics of fluency.

Narrative
I write their conclusions on the chart paper, commenting, "Here's what you said a fluent reader needs to be able to do: pronounce all the words automatically (automaticity), pay attention to punctuation, group words that go together in correct phrases, and read with expression." ◆

FLUENT READERS READ WITH

❑ **Automaticity:** Pronounce all the words correctly and automatically.

❑ **Punctuation:** Pay attention to punctuation.

❑ **Phrasing:** Group words that go together in phrases.

❑ **Expression:** Read expressively, as though you were talking.

---

6 STEP SIX

Let students hear the example of a fluent reader and have them list characteristics of fluent reading.

Purpose

Now that we have discussed what characteristics should be present in fluent reading, students are ready to listen for them.

Narrative

I once again direct attention to the students' copies of the example texts. "There is a second example on your paper," I say. "This is an excerpt from Sharon Creech's new book, *Replay*. This time I'm going to play a CD recording. I'd like you to listen. Be prepared to tell us what this reader does right when he reads." I play the excerpt and students listen carefully. ◆

7 STEP SEVEN

Using examples from the excerpt, review the characteristics of fluent reading you've written on the chart.

Purpose

Requiring students to identify examples of the characteristics of fluent reading prompts them to be attentive.

Narrative

After listening to the CD, I ask students to share with their neighbor examples of good reading they heard. Then I ask them to share their ideas with the class. "Phrasing," Eric says. "He put the words together the way they belonged." "He paid attention to punctuation," Brittany offers. Teacher David Jackson reminds his students, "Yes, punctuation marks are like street signs. They give you a road map. They tell you when to stop, and when to slow down." Robin raises her hand. "He read with expression." "Can you tell me what you mean by that?" I ask. "It sounded like he was talking," she says.

"Okay," I say. "Let's look at a line like that. Tell me how he read the line *Hey Sardine.*"

Robin responds, "As though someone was calling." I agree. "He said it differently from *Leo blinks and looks around.*" David Jackson again enters the conversation. "He said it like a kid would say it, instead of like an adult." "Did the other reader do that on the tape we just heard?" I ask, referring to the previous example. "No," students respond. I call their attention to the line, *Up and at 'em George,* and repeat it without expression. "Expression is like the up-and-down rhythm of your voice," I explain.

I summarize the characteristics we have discussed so far, referring to the chart we made earlier. "So we have phrasing and punctuation. We have expression—using the language as though you are speaking. Anything else?"

Nathaniel's voice pops up. "He didn't drag out the words." "What do you mean by 'dragging out the words?'" I ask. "He just said them," Nathaniel responds. I want a clearer explanation so I refer back to the tape I made. "Let's go back to my example. Remember how for the word *whimpered*, the reader said *him . . . whim . . . whimpered*. What was she doing?" "She had to sound it out," says Jennifer. "Good," I say. "She didn't know that word automatically so she had to sound it out. The reader on the CD didn't do that. As soon as they see them, fluent readers recognize the words. *Automaticity* is an important element on our list." ◆

8 STEP EIGHT

Have students do a "chain reading" of the excerpt from Sharon Creech's *Replay*.

Purpose

Reading aloud gives students an opportunity to demonstrate fluent reading. In a "chain reading," we ask them to read only one sentence, which helps relieve any stress less proficient readers might experience.

Narrative

I review the rules for chain reading. "Now we have the characteristics of a fluent reader. Let's finish up the lesson by doing a chain reading. We'll go around the circle and each person will read one sentence. Let's use the example from *Replay* since it's longer. Nathaniel, why don't you begin." Students take turns reading the selection, sentence by sentence. When the piece is finished, we end the session with a promise to continue to talk about how we can all be "fluent readers." ◆

Lesson 2

Reading Sentences Fluently

TAUGHT BY JANE SULLIVAN TO A HOME-SCHOOLED STUDENT
SEATTLE, WASHINGTON

INTRODUCTION

As teachers, we know that when students read the same words over and over, they begin to recognize them automatically. No surprise—we all know that practice makes perfect. But most students find such practice tedious unless they are motivated by a goal they find attractive. One such goal is a final performance—before their peers or even for a larger audience. And, if the audience is entertained, the motivation increases. Boys, in particular, find comedy appealing. We chose jokes as the basis for the lesson described here. How to tell a joke! Two- or three-line jokes work well, particularly for students who are not fluent readers. They are short and sweet, removing the stress that often accompanies reading long passages. Also, jokes are easy to find online and in magazines and joke books for children. The major source for the jokes I used was *Jokelopedia* by Weitzman, Blank, Green, and Wright. I also sent the boys to the Internet to find Web sites where they could find jokes.

Our purpose for this lesson was to build sight vocabulary and teach some pointers on phrasing correctly. Not every student in fifth or sixth grade needs such instruction. A lesson like this is best taught to a small group of students who need the practice. In fact, the two students I gave this lesson to were being homeschooled. We have already met Nate and know that he is a slow, halting reader. We also know that he would benefit from such a lesson. But we needed a partner for him. His brother, Joey, volunteered even though he was older than Nate and did not need the practice; Joey served as a model of fluent reading as well as a partner for Nate. Although we used only two players for this lesson, it can also be done with small groups.

PREPARATION AND MATERIALS

- Source material for jokes

- Paper or notebook for writing scripts (computers, if available)

- A camcorder for videotaping the practice sessions (although this is optional, playback does allow students to critique their own fluency.)

PROCEDURE, PURPOSE, AND NARRATIVE

1 STEP ONE

Explain the objective of the lesson: to prepare for a stand-up comedy show.

Purpose

Giving students an attractive goal motivates them to practice.

Narrative

"Okay, Nate and Joey. Do you know what a stand-up comedy routine is?" I ask. Joey answers first. "Yeah, that's when a comedian tells jokes to an audience." Nate puts in his two cents' worth. "Oh, I watched one on TV once." "Right," I continue. "Today, I'd like you to work up a comedy routine." ◆

2 STEP TWO

Have students choose a partner. Explain that they will work in pairs to create their comedy routine. They will then perform their routine in front of the class.

Purpose

Allowing students to select their own partner acts as further motivation. Of course, some guidance may be necessary to make sure that everyone has a suitable partner.

Narrative

"Sometimes comedians work alone and sometimes they work in pairs," I explain. "You two can work as partners." "Oh, yeah," interrupts Nate. "So one guy starts the joke and the other guy gives the punch line. I get it! I'll give the punch line," he says with a determined look on his face as he turns to Joey. "You both can give the punch line," I intervene. "Taking turns is a better way to do it." Nate grimaces but agrees. ◆

3 STEP THREE

Discuss the need for discretion in choosing comedy material: comedy should entertain without injuring feelings or insulting anyone.

Purpose

Students should understand that a joke should not mock specific individuals or groups of people.

Narrative

"There is one thing you need to remember," I caution. "A joke isn't a joke if it hurts someone's feelings." "I know," Nate says. "Like when you make fun of somebody 'cause he's dumb or ugly or something like that." "Right," I continue. "So, when you choose your jokes, what do you need to remember?" Joey answers this time. "That they don't insult anybody," he says knowingly. "Okay, let's get busy," I say, taking out my book of jokes. ◆

4 STEP FOUR

Provide joke books, magazines with "laugh" columns, or other appropriate materials that will help students find material for their script.

Purpose

Selecting their own material allows students to think about the difference between what's "funny" and what's "corny."

Narrative

"First you have to write your routine," I remind them. "I know some jokes," Joey says, smiling. "I'm sure you do, and I've brought this joke book with me to help you out as well." I bring out *Jokelopedia* and flip through the pages. ◆

5 STEP FIVE

Explain that each pair will select ten examples of two-line jokes to use in their routine.

Purpose

Setting time and length limits will make it easier for students to perform the routine.

Narrative

"Do we have to use your book," Joey asks. "No," I answer. "You can use other sources as well. But this book has a lot of material to choose from." "Here's one," says Nate. "Hey Joey," he reads. "What does a chip . . . chip . . . chipmunk get when it rains?" "I don't know," Joey responds. Nate smiles as he reads, "It gets wet, silly." "That's the way to do it," I say, clapping. "Now can you find some more like that? And with practice," I say, alluding to Nate's hesitation on the word *chipmunk*, "you'll read those jokes even better." ◆

6 STEP SIX

Give students time to locate and write down the jokes they want to use.

Narrative

The two boys page through the book finding jokes they like. "Can I see if I can find some on the Internet?" Joey asks. I nod and he disappears, reappearing ten minutes later with a printout in his hand. "I found some," he announces, handing me the paper. Soon they have found the required ten jokes. ◆

7 STEP SEVEN

Once the material is chosen, explain how the routine might work: One partner reads the first line, the other partner reads the second line, and then the first partner reads the punch line.

Purpose

Providing a model for students to follow makes it easier for them to write their scripts.

Narrative

Using my computer, I show the boys how they will set up the joke in script format. "Take a look at this," I say. "This is how you will set up your script." I point to the screen where I have written a sample joke:
Nate: Hey Joey, what's black and white and red all over?

Joey: I don't know, Nate. What is black and white and red all over?
Nate: A newspaper, Joey. Get it? ◆

8 STEP EIGHT

Show students a second way they might do the routine.

Purpose

Providing several different examples gives students choice and shows them how to vary their routines.

Narrative

"Here's another way you might try," I say, writing out this version:
Nate: Hey Joey, what's black and white and red all over?
Joey: A newspaper, Nate. A newspaper's black and white and everybody reads it!

"Right," Nate says. "That way the other guy finishes the joke. Hey, I like that!" "You can use either way," I point out. "What you want to do is set the jokes up so that you each get a laugh. And don't forget," I remind them, "you need to pause after you tell your joke to give the audience a chance to laugh." "That's if they think the joke's funny," Joey remarks. ◆

9 STEP NINE

Ask students if they can think of other ways to vary the presentation. Point out that they can switch roles—i.e., alternate who delivers the punch line.

Purpose

Asking for suggestions gives students the opportunity for input.

Narrative

"Can you think of any other ways to tell your jokes?" I ask. "You could have the second guy give the wrong answer," Nate offers. "Then the first guy could say, 'No, dummy!' and give the right answer." "Don't call me a dummy," Joey says, poking Nate. I intervene. "Neither one of you is a dummy," I remind them. "So, you won't use that word—but you could say something like 'Wrong!', and give the right answer." Nate mimics me. "Wro-o-o-ng!" We move on. ◆

10 STEP TEN

Have students select five of the ten jokes they have chosen. They might want to use a four-line joke to vary the routine.

Purpose

Keeping the routine short avoids putting stress on less fluent readers.

Narrative

"Let's get going," I say. "Look through the jokes you have and pick five of the best ones." Nate seems surprised. "We're only gonna do five? It'll be over before we start." "Five is enough to begin with," I say. "You can always add more if you think your act is too short!" ◆

11 STEP ELEVEN

Have students write their scripts. (If possible, students should type their script on a computer and print out copies for each partner.) Point out that they can alter the jokes they've selected—put their own spin on them.

Purpose

Students will find their routine easier to read if the jokes are all on one page and printed out. This format also allows them to make changes in order to add their own voice to the jokes.

Narrative

"Okay, I think you're ready to write," I say. "Why don't you take the list of jokes and decide what format you want to use. Sometimes one of you should have the punch line, sometimes the other. Then, write it down that way. Make the joke your own. Change the words if you want. Make the words fit your routine." "Can we use the computer?" asks Nate. "Sure," I say. "Then you can make a copy for each of you." Nate frowns. "Don't we have to memorize the jokes?" "No, Nate," I reply. "This is a reading lesson. So I want you to read the script when you perform." "Can we memorize it if we want to?" Joey asks. "Yes," I say. "But I don't want you to spend a whole lot of time memorizing. Have the script in your hand so you can use it if you need it."

The two boys put their heads together to map out their plan. When one joke they want to use does not fit the pattern, I show them how they can change it into a two-reader dialogue. Joey enters each joke on the computer until the routine is complete. ◆

12 STEP TWELVE

Make copies of the script. Then, using highlighters of two different colors, have students highlight their own lines.

Purpose

Highlighting their lines allows students to identify their reading parts more easily.

Narrative

"We're done," Nate announces, waving two copies of the script he has printed out. "Not quite," I tell him. I hand each boy a highlighter. "Before we begin to practice," I explain, "I want you to take these highlighters and highlight each line you will read.

So, Joey, you'll highlight all the Joey lines. Nate you will . . . " I pause, waiting. "Highlight all the Nate lines," he says, finishing my sentence. The two get started coloring their own lines. ◆

13 STEP THIRTEEN

After students practice several times, have them perform the routine while you videotape it. Play the video for them and allow them to critique the fluency of their performance.

Purpose

Videotaping their performance gives students an opportunity to identify places where they need to work on their fluency.

Narrative

"Okay," I say. "I'll give you five minutes to practice. Then I want to tape your performance, okay?" "We're gonna be on TV?" Nate asks. "Hey, we'll be famous!" "Not quite," I point out. "The tape doesn't leave this room. It's for you to watch so you can see how you can do it better. So, start practicing." The two boys read their scripts while I listen in without comment.

When they're ready, I turn on my camcorder and they perform their routine. Afterward, I play back each joke, I stop the tape, and ask them what they think. After the second joke, Nate comments. "I did the first joke really good," he says. "But, I could've done better on that one." I agree. "You stumbled over the word *cockatoo*. Say it a few times." After several tries, he pronounces the word without hesitation. We move on. ◆

14 STEP FOURTEEN

Guide students to consider the best way to deliver the line, i.e., with the most appropriate speed, enunciation, and phrasing.

Purpose

Modeling with discussion *shows* rather than *tells* students how to perform.

Narrative

"So," I say when we have finished viewing the routine, "what did you notice that was good about your performance? Could you understand every word?" Joey responds first. "I could have gone a little slower. Sometimes *I* didn't understand what I said."

"Right," I agree. "We think we're talking slowly, but we get nervous and speed up. You need to take your time." "I didn't always put the words together," Nate said. "We call that phrasing, Nate. I think that happened when you came to a word you weren't sure of. You need to practice a little more and that won't happen." "Sometimes, we rushed," said Joey. "That's another good point," I say. "You need to give the audience time to laugh. You want to do it again?" They both nod and reach for their scripts. ◆

15 STEP FIFTEEN

Give students time to practice their routine. As they practice, circulate and listen, but provide input only when necessary.

Purpose

Allowing students to practice independently while monitoring their progress provides opportunities for scaffolding.

Narrative

The two boys read their lines while I play the part of the audience, laughing to give them a cue to pause between jokes. ◆

16 STEP SIXTEEN

When, in your judgment, students are ready, gather an audience and give them the opportunity to perform.

Purpose

The performance brings the lesson to closure.

Narrative

After several tries, Nate, Joey, and I agree that they are ready for a real audience. We gather family around. Since they are at home, the boys wait behind the living room drapes. I introduce them: "May I present the comedy team of Nate and Joey," I announce, drawing the improvised curtain apart. The two boys perform their routine and bow as the audience applauds. ◆

Lesson 3

Using Readers Theater as a Method for Developing Fluency

Taught by Jane Sullivan in David Jackson's fifth-grade class
Upper Township Elementary School, Upper Township, N.J.

INTRODUCTION

Readers Theater is a well-known technique for developing students' fluency skills. The students are divided into groups, provided with a script, assigned parts, and then perform before an audience. No props are used in the activity, nor do the readers act with gestures. They convey the meaning to the audience with their voices alone. For younger students, simple picture books, such as Margaret Wise Brown's *Runaway Bunny*, can easily be converted into a Readers Theater script. Older students can be taught how to convert dialogue from a novel into play-script format.

First, I demonstrated how to turn dialogue from a story into a play script. Groups of students then chose a section of a book they were reading and turned them into scripts. Then, in sequence, they performed their Readers Theater pieces. Each of the performances was taped and burned onto a DVD. Finally, the class viewed the DVD, and using a rubric created from the list of fluency characteristics students had identified in Lesson 1: How Do We Recognize Fluency (page 20), each student critiqued his or her own oral reading. Since this lesson was carried out over several days, I have described each of the four sections of the lesson separately.

Section One: Studying the Format of a Readers Theater Script

PREPARATION AND MATERIALS NEEDED

- A novel appropriate for the age group (In this lesson, I used Lois Lowry's *Number the Stars*.)
- Transparencies and copies of a sample script from the book you will use
- Chart paper to record steps students will follow in creating their own scripts

PROCEDURE, PURPOSE, AND NARRATIVE

1 STEP ONE

Explain the purpose of the lesson: to dramatize parts of the story we are reading. Introduce the activity as "Readers Theater."

Purpose

Explaining the purpose of the lesson provides a framework for the technique students will learn.

Narrative

"You've seen books you've read—*Harry Potter*, for example—made into movies," I say. "Well, that's a bit like what we're going to be doing for the next few days. We call it Readers Theater. Let me show you the procedure we'll follow." ◆

2 STEP TWO

Show students a transparency of the prepared example script. Discuss the format you used to create this script.

Purpose

Showing a model of what students are expected to do is always better than simply "telling."

Narrative

I put the transparency I've prepared on the overhead, revealing only two lines of dialogue to introduce, and model the format. I point to Annemarie's line: *Annemarie: I'll race you to the corner, Ellen.* "Anyone recognize that line?" Mia's hand goes up. "It's from the beginning of *Number the Stars*," she says. I nod. "But, see how I've written it," I point out. "That's different from the way it was in the book, isn't it?" Derrick says. "It's like a play."

I respond with a nod. "This is a script we would use for Readers Theater. Let me show you how I

SCRIPT FORMAT AND EXAMPLE

Format:

Name (stage direction): words

Example:

Annemarie: I'll race you to the corner, Ellen.

Ellen (laughing): No, you know I can't beat you. . . .

---

wrote it. Afterward, you'll do one of your own. Take your copy of *Number the Stars* and turn to page one." I wait while students find that page. "Now, find the names of the characters on that page." Erica's hand goes up and at my nod, she names the characters: "Annemarie and Ellen." "Good, Erica," I acknowledge. "Now, I want you to find the words that Annemarie and Ellen said—so the punctuation you will look for will be . . ." Hannah finishes my sentence, "Quotation marks." "Let's see how I did it." I point to each part of the line in the script and read it out loud, including the punctuation marks:

"*Annemarie . . . colon . . . space . . . I'll race you to the corner . . . comma . . . Ellen . . . period.* You'll notice that I didn't use any other words—just dialogue," I say as I underline the parts and write underneath the line: *name-colon-words.* ◆

3 STEP THREE

Explain how to include stage directions. Point out that they should refer only to the voice. No other actions are allowed.

Purpose

As they prepare to write a Readers Theater script for fluency practice, students need to know how to include directions about vocal expression, as well as how to write the dialogue. For this type of script, we don't use gestures in the stage directions; the expression they use as they read must convey the meaning.

Narrative

"What if it says *shouting* or *whispering*?" Hannah asks. "Good thinking, Hannah," I respond. "You can put an adverb or a phrase in parentheses after the character's name to show *how* the character spoke. See how I did that here." I point to the next line with the word *laughing* in parentheses. "But don't include any actions, like *waving her hand* or *stamping his feet.* In Readers Theater, you just say the words—you don't make any gestures!"

"So, we can say *shouting* but we can't say *standing up* or *running*?" asks Stephanie. "That's right," I answer. "This will keep us focused on the way our voices can show how the characters are feeling." ◆

4 STEP FOUR

Explain the role of the narrator.

Purpose

Students need to know how to assign necessary description to the role of narrator.

Narrative

I uncover the beginning of the script on the transparency—the part of the narrator. "So that our audience will be able to imagine the setting," I say, "we sometimes use a character we call the narrator. That character reads any description that helps us understand what is going on. Look at the back cover of your book. Read that summary to yourselves."

I wait while the students read the paragraph. "Now," I say, "look at the words I've assigned to the narrator. What do you see?" Hannah responds first. "You used these words and gave them to the narrator," she says, reading: *Their life in Copenhagen, Denmark, is filled with school, food shortages, and the Nazi soldiers marching in their town.* "Yes," I acknowledge. "What else do you notice?" "You say where the girls are going," offers Mia. I agree. "Yes, I need to tell my audience when and where the action is taking place. So, put a narrator in your script to tell us the time and place and any other description your audience will need to know. But keep the narrator's part short." ◆

SCRIPT EXAMPLE WITH NARRATOR INTRODUCTION

Number the Stars, Chapter One: Why Are You Running?

Characters: Narrator, Annemarie, Ellen, Kirsti, Nazi soldier

Narrator: Annemarie and Ellen, best friends, are walking home from school with Annemarie's little sister, Kirsti, one day. The time is 1943 and their lives in Copenhagen, Denmark, are filled with school, food shortages, and the Nazi soldiers marching in their town.

Annemarie: I'll race you to the corner, Ellen. Ready?

Ellen (laughing): No! You know I can't beat you—my legs aren't as long. Can't we just walk, like civilized people?

---

5 STEP FIVE

Ask a student to demonstrate reading the lines with expression.

Purpose

Providing an example increases students' retention of the procedures you've discussed.

Narrative

"Let's practice reading my script now. Who will read the first line?" I ask. Steph raises her hand. "Read it the way you think Annemarie would say it," I direct. Steph reads the whole line, "*Annemarie: I'll race you to the corner, Ellen.*" "Close, Steph, but—" Before I can finish, Steph realizes what she did: "I shouldn't have said *Annemarie*." "Well, let's see what we can do with the next line," I say, pointing to the next line on the transparency. *Ellen (laughing): No, you know I can't beat you.* "What is different about this line?" Mia volunteers: "You have to laugh as you read the words." "Yes," I say, "because I put in a stage direction. Let's see what Lois Lowry wrote in the book. Turn to page one again." We look at the page. "She said it laughing," Derrick said, reading from the book: "*No, she said, laughing.*" I nod. "That makes it easy for me to put in that stage direction. Can you see how in Readers Theater, you use your voice—and only your voice—to let the listener know how the character feels?" The students nod in agreement and we move on. We go around the group, with students taking turns reading the lines. I am satisfied that they all understand that they read only the dialogue aloud. ◆

6 STEP SIX

Have students summarize the steps they will follow in writing scripts of their own. As they identify each step, write it on chart paper for future reference.

Purpose

Creating a chart gives students something to refer to as they work on their script. (See example below.)

Narrative

"Now, we'll form groups. Each group will create a script like the one I have here. So, let's list the steps you will follow to do that," I say. Austin begins, "You find dialogue in the story." I agree, "Yes, and I'll help you find scenes in our story that will make good Readers Theater scripts." I write Austin's step on the chart paper. "And then what?" I ask, turning back to the group. Austin continues, "And you write it like a play script." "How so?" I ask. I point to the parts I underlined in the sample script. "*Name-colon-words*," Austin reads. Mia continues: "You can put some directions in—like laughing. I combine those ideas and write step 2. "And then you read the words but not the character's name or the stage directions," Steph contributes. "And you just sit there—you can't act it out," says Sarah. "You need to practice so it sounds good," Nate adds. I list these steps on our chart as students give them to me. ◆

STEPS IN WRITING A READERS THEATER SCRIPT

Step 1: You find dialogue in the story.

Step 2: Write the dialogue as a play script: Name, any stage direction, colon, words.

Step 3: You read the words. You just sit there—you can't act it out.

Step 4: You need to practice so it sounds good.

---

7 STEP SEVEN

Conclude the lesson—and continue it at the next literacy session.

Purpose

The closure helps focus students on the next step: writing their own scripts.

Narrative

"Now that you know how to write a Readers Theater script," I say, "you should do one of your own. We can do that tomorrow, if Mr. Jackson agrees." David nods and I send students off to their next activity. ◆

Section Two: Planning a Readers Theater Script

PREPARATION AND MATERIALS NEEDED

- The same novel used in Section One
- Copies of the sample script used in Section One for the class
- The chart listing the steps for putting on a Readers Theater play created in Section One
- A list of scenes from the book you will use. The scenes should have enough dialogue and a minimum of description so that they can be converted easily into scripts. (They should take about five minutes to perform.) They should have enough roles so that each member of the group will have a part. Have more scenes than groups to ensure that each group will have a choice.

PROCEDURE, PURPOSE, AND NARRATIVE

1 STEP ONE

Recap the work the class did in the first lesson and explain that today the class will be forming groups and writing scripts.

Purpose

Students need to recall and make a connection between studying the format of the script and writing their own scripts.

Narrative

"Yesterday," I say, "I showed you how I would write a Readers Theater script." I display the transparency of the example script. "Today, I'd like you to try writing your own scripts. So, let's get into groups of five and then we'll find some dialogue you can use for your own scenes." Students scramble to change seats while David and I circulate, monitoring the formation of their groups. ◆

2 STEP TWO

Provide a list of sections of the story that students base their scripts on. Make sure there are enough speaking parts in each section—in our case, we needed five.

Purpose

Choosing appropriate material for students to use, with juicy dialogue and the right number of parts, makes it easier for them to get more out of the activity.

Narrative

Once the groups are set, I call the students to attention. "Take a look at this list of pages," I say, pointing to the transparency. "Any one of these scenes would make a good Readers Theater script. So find these pages, talk to your partners and let me know which scene you would like to do. As you tell me, I'll cross out the scene you pick so no other group can use it." Soon each group has chosen a scene. ◆

3 STEP THREE

Have one member of the group (preferably someone who can write legibly) act as scribe. The group gets to work, deciding what dialogue and stage directions, if any, they will use for their script.

Purpose

Having one member act as scribe should make the process move faster. The completed script can be copied for the other members of the group.

Narrative

"Now that you have all chosen the section you will use," I say, "you need to read it over and decide on the dialogue, the role of the narrator, and stage directions. But first, choose one group member to write out the script. Make sure that person has neat handwriting. Talk among yourselves and decide who will do that." I visit each group and make a list of the script each group is working on and the name of the scribe. ◆

4 STEP FOUR

Allow student groups to work together to create the script.

Purpose

Students benefit from opportunities to work cooperatively.

Narrative

As the groups work on their scripts, David and I circulate to give assistance where needed. We check to be sure they include all the dialogue and any necessary stage directions, and we make suggestions for the role of narrator. The scenes are short, so before long the scripts are finished and we make copies for each member of the group. "This is the end of this session," I announce. "Next time, we'll assign parts and practice our presentations. Be thinking about which part you would like to have." ◆

5 STEP FIVE

Review and edit students' scripts and allow time for the groups to gather and make the changes to create a final copy. Make copies of each group's final script.

Purpose

Polished, recopied scripts support fluent reading.

Narrative

Students submit their scripts, which David and I review. We make suggestions for revisions and editing where necessary. After the group has made revisions, we provide time for the scribe to rewrite the dialogue neatly or type it. We make copies of each group's script for the group members. ◆

Section Three: Performing the Readers Theater Script

PREPARATION AND MATERIALS NEEDED

- A copy of the revised, edited, and printed script for each member of the group
- Highlighters, one for each student
- A chart of fluency characteristics
- A camcorder
- Transparency of the sample script
- Transparency of the list of characteristics of fluent reading

PROCEDURE, PURPOSE, AND NARRATIVE

1 STEP ONE

Review the components of fluent reading.

Purpose
A review reminds students of the necessary components.

Narrative
Students are seated with their groups. Each member has a copy of his group's completed script. "Remember when we listened to those tapes," I say. "You could tell me what makes reading aloud interesting. Can you remember the list of things we need to do to read fluently?" I put up the chart we had created for that lesson (see page 23):

FLUENT READERS READ WITH

❏ **Automaticity:** Pronounce all the words correctly and automatically.

❏ **Punctuation:** Pay attention to punctuation.

❏ **Phrasing:** Group words that go together in phrases.

❏ **Expression:** Read expressively, as though you were talking.

We read the four points together. "What do we mean when we say, 'read expressively, as though you were talking'?" I ask. Eva offers the explanation: "It should sound like you're having a conversation, not reading." "That's a good way of putting it," I say. "We'll give you some time to practice. And I want you to use these four points to help each other read the parts fluently. There's one more thing I want you to do before that, though." The students wait for my next direction. ◆

2 STEP TWO

Have each student highlight the lines he or she will read aloud.

Purpose

Highlighting helps students keep track of their own lines.

Narrative

"I'd like you to do something that will make the reading a bit easier," I say. "Evan," I ask, "will you pass out these highlighters, one highlighter for each person?" When Evan finishes the task, I explain: "Take the highlighter and highlight the lines you will read. Only those lines. For example, if I were going to read the part of Annemarie in my script, I'd highlight her lines. Like this." I put up the transparency of the example script I made and highlight the line *Annemarie: I'll race you to the corner, Ellen.* "Now, you highlight all your lines." David and I circulate to make sure the students follow my directions. ◆

3 STEP THREE

Have students rehearse their lines. Remind them to use the list of fluency characteristics as a guide.

Purpose

Students will need an opportunity to practice before the actual performance.

Narrative

"Now, I want each group to practice your Readers Theater script. Here is a copy of our fluency characteristic list for each of you." I hand the papers to Mia and ask her to pass them out while I put a copy on the overhead. "Let's go over these," I say. We read each characteristic in chorus. "Now, here's what I want you to do. Read through the script. Listen to one another read the lines. When you are finished, talk about how each member read—did he or she know all the words? Pay attention to the punctuation? Group words that go together in correct phrases? Read with expression?" I point to each bullet on the chart as I review it. "Tell the member of your group what he or she did well and how he or she might read more fluently. Be specific. Then, go over the script again and see if you can do it a little better. Help one another give the best performance you can. I'll call time in about 15 minutes. Then we'll give the performances." While the groups practice, David and I set up chairs in the front of the room. We call the students together after 15 minutes and announce that it is time to begin. ◆

4 STEP FOUR

Have each group perform their Readers Theater scene in the sequence that it appears in the book. Videotape each performance.

Purpose

Performing for the class makes the activity purposeful and brings it to closure. Videotaping the performances will allow students to critique their own work later.

Narrative

"I will be videotaping each performance," I say, taking out my camcorder. "Then, next week, I'll let you see the DVD I've made and we'll talk about how fluently you read your parts. So, let's get started." I call the first group to the front of the room and ask the members to take their seats on the chairs I've arranged there.

I nod and they begin. Each group performs in order. We applaud as each group finishes its Readers Theater scene. ◆

Section Four: Critique of the Readers Theater Performance

PREPARATION AND MATERIALS NEEDED

- A DVD of the camcorder recordings made in the previous section
- Copies and a transparency of the Rubric for Assessing Fluency (page 44)

PROCEDURE, PURPOSE, AND NARRATIVE

1 STEP ONE

Explain the purpose of the rubric

Purpose

Students benefit from critiquing their own work.

Narrative

"Last week," I remind students, "I recorded your Readers Theater presentations, and over the weekend I made a DVD from that recording.

So, today, I'd like you to watch yourselves as you perform." ◆

2 STEP TWO

Explain the purpose of the rubric.

Purpose

Students need to know the function of a rubric and how they can use it to improve their work.

Narrative

"But first," I say, "I'd like you to look at that list of characteristics of a fluent reader." I point to the chart on the wall and continue. "I took each item on that list and made this rubric." I hand the papers to Derrick and ask him to pass them out. At the same time, I put a transparency of the rubric on the overhead. "What does *rubric* mean?" asks Rebecca. "I'll show you," I say.

When everyone has a copy of the rubric, I continue. "This is what we call a rubric. What do you see on this rubric that is different from our chart on fluency characteristics?" I ask. Nathaniel spies the difference first. "This has numbers from one to five next to each characteristic." "That's right," I say. "That is what makes it a rubric. You can see from the directions that each number stands for the kind of performance, from *1=very poor* to *5=excellent*. If Mr. Jackson were giving you a grade for your performance, Nathaniel, he would ask himself, 'On a scale of one to five, how well did Nathaniel do on each characteristic? Did he do poorly, average, or excellent?'"

"Is Mr. Jackson going to grade us?" Mia asks. "No," I respond. "Instead, after we look at the DVD, each of you will grade your own performance. You will rate your performance by circling the number you think you deserve. Using a rubric is a good way to learn how to do something better." ◆

3 STEP THREE

Show the video. Further explain how to use the rubric.

Purpose

Self-evaluation is an important part of learning.

Narrative

"So, we'll watch the DVD. Then, each one of you will decide how well *you* did, yourself, on each of those characteristics." "In a way," Austin says, "we're giving ourselves a grade."

"That's right," I say. "And that is a very good habit to get into. We ask ourselves, 'Can I do that better next time?' And if the answer is yes, we ask, 'How?' The rubric helps us answer that *how* question. So let's begin."

David inserts the DVD, and we all settle back to watch each of the five performances. Then we give the students time to complete the rubric. Remarks students make on their own performance—"Oh, I said that too fast" or "Oops, I forgot about that comma"—convince David and me that self-evaluation works. ◆

RUBRIC FOR ASSESSING FLUENCY

Directions: Circle the number that describes your performance best.

1 = very poor   2 = poor   3 = average   4 = good   5 = excellent

Characteristics   **Scale**

I pronounced all words correctly and automatically.	1	2	3	4	5
I paid attention to punctuation.	1	2	3	4	5
I grouped words that go together in phrases.	1	2	3	4	5
I read expressively, as though I were talking.	1	2	3	4	5

RUBRIC FOR ASSESSING FLUENCY

Directions: Circle the number that describes your performance best.

1 = very poor   2 = poor   3 = average   4 = good   5 = excellent

Characteristics   **Scale**

I pronounced all words correctly and automatically.	1	2	3	4	5
I paid attention to punctuation.	1	2	3	4	5
I grouped words that go together in phrases.	1	2	3	4	5
I read expressively, as though I were talking.	1	2	3	4	5

CHAPTER THREE

Vocabulary Building as a Path to Automaticity

The building—red brick, old, and somewhat imposing with its tall white pillars—beckons visitors to enter. Streams of children, laughing and calling to one another, file in at the sound of the bell. Teachers stand at classroom doors,

PORTRAIT OF A CLASSROOM WHERE FLUENCY MATTERS

smiling and welcoming students. "How's your mom doing, Tina?" "What's your new baby sister's name, Jake?" "Finish that project, Sam?" I smile to myself as I catch fragments of talk. I love this school, I think to myself.

I pause outside the last room, Janie Posey's fifth-grade class, and my home for the last three months. As a university professor, what I miss most is having my own classroom filled with eager young minds—but Janie has welcomed me in and I revel in the days I spend with the children. I've become sort of an unofficial literacy coach, focusing now on increasing fifth graders' fluency.

"Woo-hoo! Dr. M's here!" announces Rodney.

Twenty-two fifth graders sprawl on the worn braided rug, waving new photocopies of an adapted *Macbeth* at me.

"Awesome!" I exclaim. "You have *Macbeth*. So, what do you think? Have you read it and talked with Mrs. Posey?"

"Not only that, Dr. M., but we've picked out the parts we want to audition for—" Sasha begins.

"Yeah, we're ready to begin, now!" Eric jumps up and opens to a page marked with a sticky note. "I'm trying out for Macduff."

"Great, Eric, but why Macduff?"

"Oh, that's easy, Dr. M. My older brother was Macduff in his high school play. And I listened to him all the time, practicing and practicing his lines."

"Well, okay then," Janie nods. "Class, we need to figure auditions out. Look over the play again and be sure you know where your parts begin."

The two of us study the sign-up sheet carefully, as the room hums with energy.

"The kids are so excited, Midge. But I do have some serious reservations about Eric's choice. I had hoped he would choose stage crew or sound technician. He's artistic and loves music, but he's set on being Macduff."

"Macduff? Yikes," I respond. "He's a key character, with as much to say as Lady Macbeth."

"I know," says Janie. "Eric's such a struggling reader. Even with simple texts, he doesn't read fluently. And forget about expressively. But how can we disappoint him?"

"Hmmm . . ." I wonder. "How 'bout we let him try out today? I have a feeling that many of the students will need to work on expressive talk. And they'll all need to get in the heads of the characters, so to speak. Today's just first try-outs. Let's let Eric go ahead, and we'll see how he does."

Janie nods, "Well, okay, I guess. But I hate to lead him on."

"I hear you, but let's take a chance. If he's anywhere close, I'll gladly work extra with him," I say. Inwardly, I wonder too. Eric is struggling more with reading than anyone else in the class. During the time I've spent here, he avoids reading whenever he can. It's surprising that he's so adamant about playing this character . . .

"Come on, Dr. M. and Mrs. Posey," interrupt Ben and Chris. "We're ready!"

"Yeah, Dr. M.!" chorus three girls. "We're trying out for the witches! By the pricking of our thumbs, something wicked this way comes. Surprised, Dr. M.? We took the play home for the last two nights and we already know our lines."

"Okay, okay!" I say with a laugh. "But let's begin with Macbeth and Macduff. Jared, you stand over there for Macbeth. And Eric, stand here. What scene did you pick?"

"The fight scene!" exclaim both boys.

"All right, but no fighting today. We're only listening to you read your parts. Begin when you're ready." Janie and I settle into our director chairs, clipboards in hand. "Everyone else sit back and listen. Imagine the scene . . ."

The class quiets, all eyes on the two boys. As Jared searches for the page, he is brusquely pushed aside. Eric drops his script and jumps in front, pointing at the would-be Macbeth. His voice booms and he jabs the air with an imagined sword.

> *That way the noise is. Tyrant, show thy face!*
> *If thou be'st slain and with no stroke of mine,*
> *My wife and children's ghosts will haunt me still.*
> *I will strike at thou, Macbeth,*
> *Or else my sword with an unbatter'd edge*
> *I sheathe again undeeded.*

"Wow!" murmur several students. "Eric's *good!*"

Janie and I exchange surprised looks. "Eric, that was great!" Suddenly the class applauds, and Eric grins sheepishly. "Well, my Dad and I practiced over and over at home. So much, that I practically memorized it! Did I get the part?"

"Absolutely!" We laugh as Eric high-fives Ben, then Chris, then everyone.

"See what happens when you practice your reading?!" I give Eric a wink. "Sorry, E., but I couldn't resist! Congratulations, Macduff. You'll steal the show!"

In this classroom, students learn the importance of fluency in their reading not because the school mandates it but because they *want* to. These fifth graders have reason to practice because they've learned that fluent readers can instill emotion and passion into written words. Struggling readers such as Eric can become inspired to read and read again if they see the purpose. Being Macduff worked for Eric, but there exist boundless possibilities for teachers to help students tap into their particular interests and learn the power of fluency.

"Good job!" we want to cheer with Janie and Midge for students like Eric. He understands the importance of "knowing the words" in order to read fluently. And that is what this chapter is all about—instantly recognizing words and their meanings as well. And how do we do this? In *Bringing Words to Life*, Isabel Beck tells us that we need to provide "frequent rich and extended instruction" in vocabulary if we are to improve our students' reading comprehension (2002). That makes sense, since we know that automaticity in word recognition allows students to focus on meaning.

Listening, speaking, reading, writing—from birth, that is the order in which we build our vocabularies. When we decide which stories to share with our students in the early grades, we usually look at the vocabulary and ask ourselves, "Will students in our class recognize these words when they hear them?" In other words, we think about their listening and speaking vocabulary. And, from that list we select the words we teach as "sight vocabulary." At the same time, we provide the experiences our students need so they can expand their listening and speaking vocabularies. Thus, their word knowledge grows on several levels: They build larger oral vocabularies through listening and speaking, and their sight vocabulary grows as their range of reading material becomes broader.

UPPER-GRADE VOCABULARY: A NEW CHALLENGE

In the upper grades, our focus on vocabulary shifts. Our students will meet words in their reading that may not be heard in ordinary conversation. We can be sure that our Macduff, Eric, never heard such words as *sheathe* or *tyrant* around the lunch table. But he knew those words because, as he tells us, "my dad and I practiced over and over at home." We can be equally sure that Eric and his dad talked not only about the *pronunciation* of those words but about their *meanings*, and his presentation showed that he knew them well. As readers, we need to know those meanings in order to read the text fluently.

Our vocabulary lessons in fifth grade and beyond shift slightly and take on a two-pronged approach. We not only teach students to recognize selected words on sight, we teach them strategies that help them figure out their meaning. Researchers such as Calfee and Drum (1986), and Beck, McKeown, and Kucan (2002) agree that we pass through "dimensions" as our understanding of a word grows. Some look at a word and think: "I've never seen that word before." Some will think: "I've seen that word but I cannot define it." Others will think they know what the word means. But do they? And then there are those who not only recognize a selected word but can give the correct definition (or a synonym) for it. As Beck, McKeown, and Kucan point out "one of the strongest findings about vocabulary instruction . . . is that multiple encounters are required before a word is really known." In these lessons in vocabulary, we urge teachers to provide opportunities for those "multiple encounters." It is not enough to present a list of words and assign students to write down their definitions. Our goal should be to build an environment in which word study catches our students' interest, piques their curiosity, and creates a passion for word knowledge. The lessons in this chapter are designed to help you do that.

Boredom was not a factor for Eric because he wanted to get the part. His motivation was high! As he says, he and his father "practiced over and over." We've included suggestions for tasks that will motivate older students to expand their vocabularies.

Yet, motivation alone cannot build our students' automaticity. Eric's work became complicated when he met a word like *sheathe*. Not only was the word a new one for him, but so was the concept of *sheathing a sword*. As we read challenging texts, this happens not infrequently. We come across an unfamiliar word, look it up in the dictionary, and then cannot understand the definition. The question "What is that?" pops up. If we have already learned the concept, the new word becomes a label for that concept—Aha! *To bellow* is *to roar*! Easy enough. But what if the concept itself is a new one? That's a double task because we not only need to learn the word, we also need to have at least a vague idea about the concept. Remember when the word *Internet* did not exist in our vocabulary? Or *iPod*? Or *blogging*? (For some, who lack technology savvy, they are still a mystery!) To really learn a word, we need to understand both the concept and its label.

Most experts agree that wide reading is the most effective way to increase vocabulary. They also point out that new words should be introduced in context and that repeated use of such words moves the learner from the "I don't know" to "the correct definition is" dimension. In the lessons "Becoming Wizards of Words" and "From Page to Stage: Fluency in More Difficult Texts," we make sure that we introduce "new" words in a meaningful sentence or with a synonym. We also include actual examples or illustrations, when possible, to help students grasp the meaning solidly. Finally, we emphasize being selective in the vocabulary you teach in these lessons. Allen (1999) recommends that when we choose vocabulary to target, we need to consider the *importance* of the words to the reader, the *frequency* of their use, and their *applicability in other contexts*. How often will our students encounter the word *prioritize* or *vehicular* as opposed to *antenna* or *digital*? (Words, by the way, I found on the op-ed page of today's newspaper.) How long will they remember the definitions, use the words in their own speech or writing, or read them in the writing of others? We chose the vocabulary in these lessons based on practical criteria: What are my students reading? What words have they themselves selected for word study? How can they share these words with their classmates?

Strategies for learning vocabulary that include repeated encounters with the new words—concept maps, word walls, use of context, word parts, definition games—have been proven to be effective techniques for expanding students' vocabularies. In *Vocabulary in the Elementary and Middle School* (2001), Dale Johnson encourages "active involvement with words" and points to Stahl's research, which found "vocabulary teaching methods that gave only definitional information did not appear to significantly improve comprehension" (p. 44). If our goal is to improve our students' fluency and ultimately their comprehension, then expanding their vocabulary through direct instruction and varied approaches must be part of our reading curriculum. Leaving growth in vocabulary to chance or copying word definitions is not an option.

With these lessons, our goal is to introduce new vocabulary strategies that can motivate students to develop a curiosity about words, and equip them with ways to satisfy that curiosity. Expanding students' vocabulary leads to automaticity in word identification, which, as we have pointed out before, is an important factor in students' ability to read fluently.

LESSONS IN THIS CHAPTER

Lesson One:
Word Detective: Techniques for Finding Word Clues in Text (page 51)
Objective: Identify the techniques authors use to define a word in context.

Lesson Two:
Learning New Vocabulary through READ-O (page 56)
Objective: Gain automaticity with reading or content-area vocabulary through repeated exposure to the words and their meanings in a bingo-style game.

Lesson Three:
Building Fluency in More Difficult Texts: Moving Words From Page to Stage (page 61)
Objective: Practice using new vocabulary in an interactive prereading exercise that helps students internalize word meanings and gain automaticity.

Lesson Four:
Becoming "Wizards of Words" (page 69)
Objective: Practice using new vocabulary from a selected text in a high-context lesson; learn to use an interactive word wall to support ongoing practice with the words.

Lesson One

Word Detective: Techniques for Finding Word Clues in Text

TAUGHT BY JANE SULLIVAN IN DAVID JACKSON'S FIFTH-GRADE CLASS
UPPER TOWNSHIP ELEMENTARY SCHOOL, UPPER TOWNSHIP, N.J.

INTRODUCTION

When using less common words in their texts, authors often provide their definitions, sometimes overtly, sometimes subtly. We need to teach our students to be on the alert for such clues. That is the purpose of this lesson: to learn the techniques authors use to define a word through example or description.

PREPARATION AND MATERIALS NEEDED

- Examples of the various types of clues found in text. (Examples for this lesson are taken from Sharon Creech's novel *Bloomability*.)

PROCEDURE, PURPOSE, AND NARRATIVE

1 STEP ONE

Introduce the focus of this lesson: How authors leave clues to the meaning of words that we might not know.

Purpose

Students may not be used to thinking of the subtleties of the author's craft as extending outside the realm of plot and storytelling.

Narrative

I introduce the lesson topic. "You know, Sharon Creech is a very smart author. She knows her audience. So when she wants to use a word that her readers may not know, she'll often give us a clue that will help us understand it. Why do you think smart authors do that?" Chris answers first. "So we don't have to run to a dictionary every time we come to a word we don't know?" he asks. I nod. ◆

2 STEP TWO

Introduce the topic of the lesson, using an illustration from reading students are or have been engaged in. Introduce the first example of clues in the text.

Purpose

Beginning the lesson with this example helps guide students through an inductive learning experience.

Narrative

"Remember when I was reading this paragraph in *Bloomability* and we came to the word *figurehead*? I asked you what it meant—what happened?" "I ran for the dictionary," admitted Tara. "Yes, you did, Tara, and that wasn't wrong. But there was a quicker way to find the meaning."

I put a transparency up and read the example: *"I thought maybe she was a figurehead, like the queen of England. And maybe she really didn't do anything."* "What are the clues here that hint at what a figurehead is?" I ask. Tara answers, *"Maybe she didn't do anything."* "And do you remember what definition you found in the dictionary, Tara?" I ask. She pauses and then remembers. "It said a figurehead was *a chief or a leader in name only.*" "Yes," I agree. "And look at what Sharon Creech tells us." I underline *queen of England* and *she really didn't do anything.* "So, she has given us two clues. What does *queen of England* tell us?" I ask. Chris answers. "*Queen* is an example of a figurehead. She doesn't really do anything," "Okay," I agree.

"So, sometimes, an author will give us an example. The queen of England has no real power to make decisions—a figurehead has no real power to make decisions. And in case we don't know that about the queen of England, Creech gives us a second kind of clue. She actually explains the word—*she really didn't do anything.*" Jessica raises her hand. "In our science book, a new word like that is in bold and they put the meaning in parentheses." "Yes, I say. "You'll find that, but mostly only in textbooks and nonfiction books." ◆

3 STEP THREE

Provide practice in the strategy: defining a word by finding an example, especially one that draws a comparison with something more familiar.

Purpose

Repeating the exercise reinforces the technique.

Narrative

"So let's see if you can figure out the meaning of this word." I move the paper on my transparency down to expose the next lines:
The trees swayed in the wind, like dancers moving to music.
"If you know the meaning of *sway*

already, don't answer." I caution. "For the rest of you, what clue hints at the meaning of *sway*?" Hannah raises her hand. "Dancers move back and forth to music," she thinks aloud. "So *sway* must mean back and forth." I nod and ask: "What word do you see in our two examples, Hannah, that points to that clue?" She examines both examples and offers the word *like*. "Yes." I respond. ◆

4 STEP FOUR

State the strategy of "using an example" as one way to determine the meaning of a word.

Purpose

Restating the strategy helps reinforce the procedure.

Narrative

I summarize. "So, using the word *like* to link the new word with an example is a flag that tells us a clue is coming. This is one of the strategies an author might use to help us with word meanings. As good readers, we want to add new words to our vocabulary. Authors are our friends when they help us do that. We need to be on the lookout for that clue." ◆

5 STEP FIVE

Introduce a second clue authors use: context and parts of speech.

Purpose

Alert students that an example of a different type of clue will be introduced.

Narrative

"Let's look at another clue authors might give us." I put up the following example on the overhead: *And, since he doled out his insults to everyone in turn, it was easier to take it when he zeroed in on you.* "There are two words in this example that may be new to you," I continue. "Even if we don't know the meanings, we can probably use the context and part of speech to help us figure it out." ◆

6 STEP SIX

Provide the example and guide students through the discovery process.

Purpose

Having students use prior knowledge encourages them to make the connection between what they know and what they're learning.

Narrative

"What part of speech are *doled* and *zeroed*?" I ask. "Who wants to try this one?" Evan raises his hand. "Verbs?" I nod in agreement. "How do you know that, Evan?" He shrugs. "They both end in *–ed* and verbs end in

—ed?" "Good guess," I say. "But we can't be sure by just looking at the word. Look at where it is in the sentence." Erica responds: "They both follow *he* and they're actions, so Evan's probably right." "Good detective work, Erica," I remark. "Now, think a bit further. Let's use the rest of the sentence. Do we 'dole out' something or someone?" Chris answers this time. "Insults. We dole out insults. And we dole them out to someone." I give another prompt. "Can someone think of another word that would fit into that sentence? He *hmmm* insults to everyone." Hands fly up. "Says." "Calls out." "Gives."

I clap for attention. "Okay, you have given me some good examples that make sense. Do you see how context and the part of speech narrow the possibilities? Let's see if we can do that with our next example, *zeroed*." Derrick tries this one. "If everyone is insulted, you're going to be included, so *zeroed in* might mean *picked on*." "Good try, Derrick," I say. "Anyone have any other ideas?" "Zero is like a bull's-eye, so it might mean *aimed at*." That was from Stephanie. "Good thinking, too, Stephanie. So now we have two possibilities: *pick on* or *aim at*. Both make sense. I read the sentence with the substitutions: "*It was easier to take it when he aimed at and picked on you.* How does that sound?" A chorus of "yeahs" arises. ◆

7 STEP SEVEN

Provide another example of using parts of speech and context.

Purpose
Repeating the exercise reinforces learning.

Narrative
"Let's try another one," I say, putting another example on the overhead: *I was fingering the ends of my scarf.* "Let's look at this phrase first." I point to the words *was fingering*. "What part of speech is *was fingering*?" "That's easy," says Austin. "Verb." "Okay," I agree, "but is *finger* usually a verb?" "It's a noun," says Jessica. "*Finger* is a noun."

"So, are you telling me that you can take a noun and make it a verb?" I ask. "Maybe it means point to with your finger," Hannah suggests. "Hmmm. Good idea. Anyone else?" "She could be touching the end of her scarf, too," Mia suggests. "Like this." And she rubs her finger against the edge of her blouse. "I like that better," Erica offers, "because it says *was fingering*. That kind of means she kept doing it." "You are such good detectives," I say. "You are correct, Erica. When we use *finger* as a verb, we mean touching or rubbing." ◆

8 STEP EIGHT

Summarize the types of clues that authors use and have students collect examples of each.

Purpose

Restating the strategy helps reinforce the procedure so that students can apply it independently.

Narrative

"So we now have two techniques authors use to help us learn new words: What are they?" I put the first example on the overhead. Derrick remembers: "Giving us examples of what the word means." "And the second strategy we can use?" I ask. This time Jessica answers. "Using the part of speech and the other words in the sentence to help figure it out." I repeat the answers. "Yes. Using the text and part of speech is one strategy. Using examples the author gives is another strategy—two ways to be word detectives." I write the examples of these strategies on chart paper.

After teaching this lesson, David and I suggest to students that they use sticky notes to "collect" new vocabulary as they read. We ask them to use the following to search for clues: the context, part of speech, and possible examples that draw comparison. Then they can write what they think the meaning of that word is. As part of reading discussion, students will share the words they have collected and the meanings they've come up with. We remind students that knowing the meaning of words helps them to read fluently and makes it easier to understand what the author is saying. ◆

LEVELING THE LESSON

In this lesson, we used examples as well as general context and parts of speech as clues to determine word meaning. With younger students, you might introduce only one strategy at a time. A follow-up exercise connecting reading with writing might have students using such vocabulary clues in their own writing.

Lesson Two

Learning New Vocabulary
Through Read-O

TAUGHT BY JANE SULLIVAN IN DAVID JACKSON'S FIFTH-GRADE CLASS
UPPER TOWNSHIP ELEMENTARY SCHOOL, UPPER TOWNSHIP, NJ

INTRODUCTION

We teachers need to encourage wide reading as a route to vocabulary growth that supports automaticity. But we also need to encourage vocabulary growth more directly by helping students collect new words and by devoting time to activities that will reinforce those words' definitions. Read-O, patterned after the game of bingo, lends itself to reinforcing the meanings of words. And it's enjoyable, too. Playing the game several times with the same vocabulary words provides the repetition students need to quickly recognize the words and understand their meanings.

Before introducing the game, I prepared the materials, choosing words from their reading that I judged to be new to at least some of the students in the class. Ultimately, I wanted the students themselves to collect words from their reading. Since students were already working together in reading circles, we used those groups to reduce the number of words each member needed to contribute to the game each group created. This approach also provided an opportunity for students to help one another. Students who are less able readers also had a chance to contribute to the project. In the follow-up lessons, students used the words their group collected to create Read-O cards. Members of each group first played the game with their own cards, then exchanged their cards with another group.

Not all the words listed will be new vocabulary to every student. That is not a primary goal of this lesson. First, being introduced to 25 new words is a challenging, if not a frustrating, experience for any reader. Second, students who know the definition can help students for whom the word is new, which teaches students to work cooperatively. Activities such as Read-O allow students to learn in an atmosphere of play and relaxation.

PREPARATION AND MATERIALS NEEDED

- A list of 25 words that will be used in the Read-O game displayed on chart paper or an overhead transparency (the words should be drawn from recent reading students have done—literature group books, class magazines, or subject textbooks, for example)

- Read-O game board (a bingo-type 5-by-5 grid filled in with the 25 vocabulary words) for each student. (While the same words are used within a given column, their order varies.)

- A large replica of one of the Read-O game boards (on an overhead transparency or chart paper) to be used as the master card

- A set of "caller" cards (3-by-5 index cards work well). For each word on the list, make a card with the word and its definition written on it, along with a suggested context.

- Small squares of paper large enough to cover a word on the Read-O card.

PROCEDURE, PURPOSE, AND NARRATIVE

1 STEP ONE

Introduce the purpose of the lesson: to play a game like bingo, but with words instead of numbers.

Purpose

Tapping students' background knowledge helps prepare them for the activity structure and focus.

Narrative

"We've been talking about the importance of learning the meanings of new words," I say. "Today, I'd like to share with you a game that will help you with vocabulary. We'll call this game Read-O. Look familiar?" I display a large chart of the Read-O game board that I've pasted to the blackboard. Rebecca raises her hand. "It looks like bingo," she says. I nod. "It does indeed. It is a little different, though. Let's see how it works." ◆

R	E	A	D	O
gigantic	remain	opportunity	slash	pound
chalet	clunk	vanish	efficient	bolt
portrait	ghastly	FREE	squabbling	luggage
fade	lure	departure	bun	sturdy
adaptable	domed	foreign	nibbling	vast

2 STEP TWO

Explain the rules of the game (see below), using the model Read-O game board to demonstrate each step of the game.

Purpose

A combination of telling and showing makes the explanation clearer.

READ-O CALLER'S CARD

Column R

Definition: Very large

Context: He had a [blank] lump on his head.

Answer: Gigantic

Narrative

I point to the letters R-E-A-D-O on the game board. "See," I say. "Five letters, just as in bingo. But instead of numbers under each letter, what do we have?" Evan raises his hand and calls out "Words!" I nod. "Yes. And later I'll give each of you a Read-O game board with all these words on it. Will each game board be exactly the same?" This time Chris answers. "They couldn't be. Otherwise, we'd all win the game at the same time!" "Good thinking, Chris. Let's see another way our game differs from bingo."

I show them the pack of cards I have made up. "These are the cards the caller will use for the game. So what do you think I've written on

RULES OF READ-O

The game follows the rules of traditional bingo:

1. Each player makes a game board, filling each column with a specific set of words, but writing them in a random order.

2. The caller selects a card from the pack.

3. The caller reads the letter indicating the column in which the player can find the word. The caller then reads the definition of the word and its context, as written on the card, e.g., "Column R. Very large. He had a [blank] lump on his head." (The word *blank* acts as a place holder for the word being defined.)

4. Players find the word that fits and cover it with a marker.

5. The first player to cover a line of words, vertically, horizontally or diagonally, calls out "Read-O" and is declared the winner of the game.

6. Different patterns may be used to vary the game: X (two diagonals), L (first column, last row), and so on.

these cards?" Eva responds this time. "The words?" "That's a good guess, Eva," I say, "but, remember, this is a game to help remember definitions." Mia catches on quickly. "The cards have the definitions written on them," she calls out, "and we have to find the word on the card that matches the definition." "Exactly," I say. "And how do we win a game?" "We need to cover a column or a row or a diagonal," Evan responds. "Good," I reply. "You know all the rules already." ◆

3 STEP THREE

Using the model Read-O game board and several caller's cards (see examples on pages 57 and 58), demonstrate the role of caller. Choose a student to be a player. Call out several definitions and have the student cover the correct word on the model Read-O card so students can see how the game is played.

Purpose

Demonstrating will clarify the procedure for the group. Inviting students to join in the demonstration helps the teacher judge if the explanation was clear enough.

Narrative

"So," I say, holding up the card I've picked. "We'll call these caller cards. On this caller card, I've written a definition of one of the words on the Read-O game board, here." I point to the R column on my Read-O game board and then read the caller's card: "*Column R. Very large. He had a* blank *lump on his head.* What word in the R column would that definition fit?" I ask. Evan finds the word first: "*Gigantic.*" I hand Evan a sticky note, saying "So, Evan, cover the word *gigantic* on the game board."

Then, I select a second card, point to column A, and read: "*Column A. Chance. He's looking for the right* blank. Can you find that word, Eva, and cover it?" I ask. Eva quickly locates *opportunity* in the third column and covers it with a sticky note. I ask, "Are there any questions?" Erica raises her hand. "Are we all going to play?" "Yes," I respond, "but first, let's finish this game and see how long it takes to win Read-O." I invite Eva to take over the role of caller, and we finish up quickly. ◆

4 STEP FOUR

Distribute the Read-O cards and paper markers. Explain that now, all the students play Read-O.

Purpose

Having students play the game individually will ensure that all students understand the procedure.

Narrative

I give out the Read-O game boards I have prepared, along with the squares of paper that will act as markers. I take a few minutes to review the procedure. "You all have the same words on each column of your card," I explain, "but the order is different. I'll read the definition from my caller card. You find the word in that column and cover it. I'll ask one of you to give me the word I defined. Then, I will circle the word on my Read-O master card chart to help you find it. Once we identify the word, you'll need to find it in the column on your card and cover it with these pieces of paper. Whoever covers all the words in a column or row or diagonal first should call out *Read-O.* Then we'll check the words again to be sure you really are the winner." I begin to call out definitions, and we continue with the game until Sasha jumps from her seat and shouts, "Bingo, I mean Read-O!" We review her answers and determine that she's identified all the words in one of the rows correctly. "Good job, Sasha," I say. "Now, let's mix up these caller cards and start again." We play the game several times and end the session with a promise to continue the game next time. ◆

FOLLOW-UP LESSONS

Students gathered in their reading groups of four or five to make their own set of Read-O cards for a new vocabulary list. Each group used the book the students were reading and worked together to create a list of 25 words, their definitions, and a phrase or sentence to use as an example. I provided each group with a form made up of three columns and a sample entry (see below).

David gave students several school days to fill out these charts. Then he collected the lists and edited them for spelling and accuracy. Each group was then ready to create caller cards and game boards. I showed students how to create the game boards by listing words for each of the five columns. Each student was responsible for writing the words in one of the five columns and then varying the order for each card. Finally, the students played Read-O with their new cards in their own groups. We gave them several opportunities to play in order to practice and reinforce the words.

FORM FOR COLLECTING READ-O VOCABULARY WORDS

Word	Definition	Context
Gigantic	Very large	He had a [blank] lump on his head.

Lesson Three

Building Fluency in More Difficult Texts: Moving Words From Page to Stage

TAUGHT BY MIDGE MADDEN IN KATHY CARHART'S FIFTH-GRADE CLASS
WILLIAM WINCHESTER ELEMENTARY SCHOOL, WESTMINSTER, MD.

INTRODUCTION

When students in fifth and sixth grades read more difficult texts, the synchrony between their speaking and reading vocabularies lessens. Students encounter words they have not yet heard and words that represent concepts they have not yet learned. How, then, do we help them when they're confronted with difficult vocabulary? How do we move older students from halting, puzzled readings to smooth, polished performances that evidence both fluency and understanding?

Teachers have long used the practice of introducing vocabulary before reading a new text. Commercial reading programs select words to preteach for each of their texts and suggest ways to present them to students, yet most such activities are teacher directed, often requiring students to listen to definitions or use the dictionary to determine meanings. Students rarely interact with new vocabulary in ways that might help them to internalize the words and make them their own. The following lesson does exactly that—students not only encounter the unfamiliar vocabulary but engage in collaborative writing and performance that encourages "owning" the new words and fosters automaticity.

PREPARATION AND MATERIALS NEEDED

- Copies of the sample texts for the class (This lesson uses the first two chapters from *Crispin* by Avi.)

- Eight to ten sentence strips with phrases from the sample text that have unfamiliar and difficult vocabulary. (See preparation note, Step 2, page 63.)

- Clipboard, paper, and pencil for a designated writer in each group of three or four students

PROCEDURE, PURPOSE, AND NARRATIVE

1 STEP ONE

Introduce the purpose of the lesson as twofold: to learn new vocabulary words by creating and performing fictitious tales and to begin reading a new novel by Avi.

Purpose

When students understand the rationale behind the lesson, they better understand directions and become more easily and successfully engaged.

Narrative

Holding a copy of the book in my hands, I say, "Today we're going to begin reading a new book in our literature circles. It's called *Crispin: The Cross of Lead.* Anyone want to take a guess at what the title means?" Rodney's hand shoots up. "I think Crispin is that kid's name, Dr. M." "Good guess!" I reply. "We'll read today to see if you're right. But before we begin, there are some tough words in this novel and some new concepts for you. The story takes place in 14th-century medieval England. Listen while I read part of the front cover flap to you."

I read the opening paragraph, which sets the scene and informs students that the main character, a 13-year-old boy, finds himself suddenly with no home, no family, and no possessions. "What happened to him?" asks Elizabeth. "I'm curious too," I respond, "But first, let's take a look at some phrases and new vocabulary from the first two chapters. That way when you begin reading yourselves, you'll have a better understanding of what 14th-century England was like." ◆

VOCABULARY HIGHLIGHTED IN PHRASES
EXCERPTED FROM THE FIRST TWO CHAPTERS OF *CRISPIN.*

Wrapped in a gray <u>shroud</u>

They had <u>shunned</u> my mother

<u>Astride</u> his horse

For <u>poaching</u> a stag, he was put to death

<u>Transfixed</u> with fear, I stood rooted

<u>Ensnared</u> in brambles

---

2 STEP TWO

Post sentence strips with phrases from the text on the blackboard so that all students can see them. In a conversational way, have students offer definitions or synonyms for the words. Agree on a meaning that students will understand for each.

Note: In preparation for this part of the lesson, read the text excerpt ahead of time and select vocabulary that may be troublesome for many of the students. Choose phrases and sentence parts, not isolated words, so that students can use context to help them determine meaning. Write each phrase or word group on a sentence strip, underlining the key word.

Purpose

Introducing new words in word groups taken from the targeted text helps students make connections with the text and better remember new vocabulary.

Narrative

"Let's take a look at these phrases I've posted (see page 62). I've underlined a tricky word in each phrase. I want you guys to help me figure out the pronunciations and meanings, okay?" Students nod. I read each phrase aloud first, then have the students read with me. I reread the phrase and ask for volunteers to guess at the meaning of the underlined words.

"*Wrapped in a gray shroud.* Hmmm, anyone want to guess the meaning of *shroud?*" Jared raises his hand, "I think I know. Isn't it like a sort of cover or blanket?" "Excellent, Jared. In past times, the custom was to wrap bodies in shrouds before burial. Let's try the next word," I continue. "*They had shunned my mother.* Any thoughts?" Elizabeth offers, "Well, it doesn't sound like they, whoever they are, liked the mother. But I don't know why I think that." Andy agrees, "I think it means they don't have anything to do with the mother." "And you're right, Andy," I reply. "Let's try another. *Astride his horse.*" Rodney exclaims, "Oh, I know that one! It means he's sitting on his horse."

"Awesome," I say with a smile. "Come on, the rest of you, try this one. *For poaching a stag, he was put to death.*" "Stealing?" ventured Anna. "But killing someone for stealing a deer seems crazy." I nod, "*Poaching* does mean stealing, and I agree—something doesn't seem right here. But we don't know yet because we haven't read the book. Good thinking." I point to the fourth sentence strip and read, "*Transfixed with fear, I stood rooted.* What do you think?"

Puzzled faces answer me, so I give a hint: "He was so scared he couldn't move." "Oh, yeah! I know!" Deanna says. "It means paralyzed. Maybe he saw something so scary that he just froze." "Excellent!" I respond. "Now there's just one more. *Ensnared in brambles.*" Nate laughs, "Aw, that's easy, Dr. M., *Ensnared* means caught. Right?"

"Okay. So maybe this was easy for you but I bet it was hard for some of us. That's why we're going through these words—to help us all better understand and learn new vocabulary. What could I have done if none of you guessed the meanings of the words?" "That's easy, too," laughed Deanna. "You could simply tell us! And maybe use the word in some other sentences so we could practice hearing it and learning it." "Right on, Deanna. I think *you* could teach this lesson!" ◆

3 STEP THREE

Put students into small groups. (Select the groups ahead of time and be sure to place a proficient writer in each group.) Direct each group to find a space in the classroom where students can work together quietly.

Purpose

Preassigning groups not only saves time, but for the purposes of this lesson, ensures that groups are heterogenous and that one person in each group can write proficiently.

Narrative

"Okay, everyone. I've put you in four groups and chosen a writer, or scribe, for each group. I'll call the scribes first, then the group members. Just stand next to your scribe when I call your name." Students form groups. I say, "Good. Now each group has five minutes to find a working space in the classroom. The scribe also needs to take a clipboard, paper, and pencil." ◆

TIP Some students may need more scaffolding when you introduce the words in context in Step 2. In this case, have students make their own word-reference sheet as you discuss the word meanings. Have them write the words on a sheet of paper and make a simple note or sketch that will help them remember the meaning of each word. They can refer to these notes when they develop and write the story in the next part of the activity.

Example:
shroud: cover, like a blanket (mummy)
shunned: rejected, not popular
poached: stolen (wildlife)
transfixed: frozen, paralyzed
ensnared: caught

4 STEP FOUR

Tell students that they have 15 minutes to create a story. It can be about anything but it must contain all of the newly introduced vocabulary words, either in the given phrases or in sentences generated by the group. The scribe puts the story down on paper.

Purpose

Writing collaborative stories is a nonthreatening way to experiment with using new vocabulary words in original writing. Students debate word choices and laugh at their developing plots. All students contribute ideas. Struggling writers don't have to worry about putting their thoughts on paper.

Narrative

"Everyone ready?" I ask. Heads nod. "Okay, here's the fun part! Each group gets to create a fictitious story about anything. But you must use all of the new vocabulary that we just talked about somewhere in your story. You can either use the entire phrases or just the word in your own sentences. Oh, and you can use the new vocabulary words in any order. Scribes, you write down the story as the group tells it to you. Don't worry about spelling or handwriting—this is just some quick practice in trying out new words. You have 15 minutes to create and write." ◆

5 STEP FIVE

Move about the classroom as groups talk and generate ideas. Answer questions that arise and reiterate directions when necessary. Remind groups of the time limit. If students are engaged and need five more minutes, give them the extra time.

Purpose

It is critical to ensure that all groups understand the directions and can work independently. The teacher acts as a coach, supporting students in brainstorming ideas.

Narrative

While students are working in groups, I circle the room, stopping to check on each group's progress. "How are you doing?" I ask. "Everyone remember that you have to use all of the new words?" Heads nod and I look around the classroom. Some students sprawl on the floor; some huddle around the reading table; others lean forward around groups of desks pushed together. Scott looks up as I approach and whispers, "We're talking real quietly. We don't want anyone to steal our ideas!" "Dr. M., Dr. M., come here," urges Jared. "Listen to what we have so far. It's so cool!"

I listen and nod. "Good ideas. Now keep going and be sure all those new words make sense in your story." I smile and continue to wander around the room, providing support where needed. ◆

6 STEP SIX

Have each scribe read the story aloud to his or her group. Then explain that each group is going to perform its story. Everyone must participate in reading and performing; it's up to the group to figure out how. Give students 15 minutes to plan and practice. For groups that need help, suggest choral reading or pair reading as well as individual reading.

Purpose

Preparing to present an original story provides students with lots of practice using the new vocabulary in a very meaningful context: polishing their own performance piece. This preparation also emphasizes good oral reading skills by providing the opportunity to address expression and prosody.

Narrative

"Time's up, everyone. Now, we're going to share our stories, but we need to follow certain steps.

First, scribes read the story back to your groups. Second, each group works together to figure out how to perform its story. You can read it aloud together, in pairs, and individually, but everyone must read. Think, too, about what performing means. It's kind of like the Readers Theater that we do in book clubs, only this time you're using your own stories. You can pantomime or act out parts to go along with the reading; it's up to you. Third, practice reading and performing. You have 15 minutes."

As the groups work, I listen in to one, and notice that students are using the vocabulary words to clarify the word meanings and improve on presentation ideas. "Let's do it this way. I'll be narrator and you guys be different people in the story, okay?" Elizabeth suggests. "I'll be the dead person in the shroud," says Andy. "I won't have to say anything!" "Very funny," says Elizabeth, "but how do you know dead people are wrapped in shrouds?" "Well, silly, we talked about bodies wrapped in shrouds in the beginning with Dr. M. Guess I just inferred bodies are dead!" "Yeah, now I remember. But it doesn't matter. Dr. M. said everyone has to read something."

I circulate around the room as groups plan and practice, making sure that they all understand the task. ◆

STEP SEVEN

Each group performs its story.

Purpose

Performing original work gives purpose to writing. Students enjoy hearing each other's work and benefit from purposeful oral reading. They also hear the same words being used in different contexts.

Narrative

"Dr. M., can we go first?" Jared pleads. "Ours is really good!" "Sure," I say, beckoning them to the front of the room. Jared begins, "Well, we decided to read it all together . . . and then we'll act the story out." The group reads in unison:

There once was a man named Braveheart who was traveling through the woods. The people in his village had shunned him and he was running away. As he came to dark woods, he saw a body wrapped in a gray shroud. He was transfixed with fear. Astride his horse, he stopped suddenly. His horse reared up and threw him off. Braveheart was ensnared in brambles. He tore his way out, trying to get free. Then he walked towards the body. "Who is it?" he thought. He pulled back the shroud. It was an old man. Around his neck was a sign that read: "For poaching a stag, you must die."

Jared holds up his hand. "No applause, yet," he says. "Now we're going to act it out."

Jake (Braveheart) hops on the back of Jared (the horse). Sarah and Kristen (the brambles) entwine arms, and Rodney (the body) lies on the floor, eyes closed. Jared leaps up, Jake falls off, and Sarah and Kristen trap him in their arms. Jake struggles and pushes Sarah and Kristen away. He walks toward Rodney. He pantomimes pulling back a cover, and lifting the sign hanging on Rodney's neck. He lays the sign back down and walks slowly away. The performance ends with one word uttered by Jake: "Why?"

The class claps. "That was so good," exclaims Deanna. Others nod in agreement. I add, "And you included all of the new words in ways that made excellent sense. Good job! Who wants to go next?" The three remaining groups take turns performing. Kathy and I encourage them to point out actions that help students really grasp the meaning of a word and also to make constructive suggestions when the presentation doesn't support their understanding. ◆

8 STEP EIGHT

Students receive copies of the sample text. They read silently.

Purpose

Having been introduced to the vocabulary, students are ready to begin reading. Familiarity with new words and concepts contributes to a deeper comprehension of the story.

Narrative

"Great work, everyone," I say. "Now, I know we spent a lot of time on this activity, but I hope working with these new words will make it easier for you to understand Crispin's story. Remember, it takes place long ago, so the language will sound a little funny to you at first. Let's read the first two chapters. Keep your eyes out for the words we just learned, and make note of any other words that confuse you. We'll talk about those words and the story after you finish reading." ◆

Lesson Four

Becoming Wizards of Words

TAUGHT BY MIDGE MADDEN IN KATHY CARHART'S FIFTH-GRADE CLASS
WILLIAM WINCHESTER ELEMENTARY SCHOOL, WESTMINSTER, MD.

INTRODUCTION

What does it mean to really *know* a word? And why is knowing words critical to fluent reading? Blachowicz and Fisher (2002) contend that learning a word is akin to slowly lighting up a room with a chandelier dimmer switch. They suggest that as readers repeatedly encounter a new word, it becomes more meaningful. Readers truly learn a word—that is, make it their own—only by meeting it again and again in multiple texts and trying it out in speech and in writing. They learn new words incrementally, moving from not knowing a word to being somewhat familiar with it, and finally arriving at a deeper, internalized knowledge of the word (McKeown & Beck, 1991; Graves, 1983; Stahl, 1997). Such knowledge of new words enables readers to use them in different ways and moves them toward automaticity, comprehension, and fluency.

But how can teachers help student readers gain this richer, more flexible word knowledge? Blachowicz and Fisher (2002) argue that teachers must do two things: (1) promote wide reading with emphasis on rich exposure to new words and (2) provide opportunities for their students to interact with and use words in meaningful contexts.

The following lesson, based on Beck and Kucan's "word wizard program" (2002), provides opportunities for students to interact meaningfully with new words by inviting them to become "wizards of words." Teachers can adapt this lesson to include new vocabulary from literature or content-area subjects. The lesson that follows uses new vocabulary from an introductory science lesson that focuses on learning about the heart and modern advances in preventing heart attacks.

PREPARATION AND MATERIALS NEEDED

- A news article related to your unit of study that contains new, useful vocabulary and helpful photographs

- Excerpt from the news article, with eight to ten target vocabulary words underlined, printed on an overhead transparency

- Color copies of photographs from the article or that relate to the selected vocabulary words

- Target vocabulary words from above underlined in high-context sentences excerpted directly from the selected article or summarized from the text, and printed on an overhead transparency

- Index cards for students' definitions of the new vocabulary

- A word wizard wall on a classroom bulletin board. (Using sentence strips or cutout letters, make the heading "Word Wizards" and post it across the top of the board. Use index cards or sentence strips to write new vocabulary and definitions and post the words on the wall. Cut out small wizard hat shapes from colored paper or use star-shaped sticky notes. Place the blank cards or sticky notes in an envelope on the wizard wall for student use—see Step 9.)

PROCEDURE, PURPOSE, AND NARRATIVE

STEP ONE

State the first goal of the lesson: to introduce and determine the meaning of new vocabulary words by reading the words in context, looking them up in the dictionary, and generating definitions. State the second goal of the lesson: to introduce the word wizard wall, which encourages the learning of new vocabulary.

Purpose

Providing an overview of a lesson helps students better understand and engage more readily in the activities.

Narrative

"Today, everyone, we're beginning a new study about one of our body's systems, called the circulatory system. Any idea what the most important part of that system is?" Garrett blurts out, "Oh, Dr. M., easy! It's the heart, of course!" "Well, how did you know that?" Garrett responds, "*Grey's Anatomy* last week was all about a guy who had heart problems, and when his heart stopped, no blood could get pumped around his body."

"Good, Garrett. And you're absolutely right—the heart *is* the most important part of the circulatory system. So, we're beginning our study about the heart, why it's important, and how it works. Last night, I read a really cool article in *National Geographic* about the heart and some ways to keep it healthy. I thought I could share parts of it with you. It might be a perfect way to begin thinking about the heart and to learn some medical terms so we sound like heart specialists, or cardiologists!" ◆

2 STEP TWO

Show students the news article related to your unit of study. Talk briefly about the main point of the article. Show and discuss photographs.

Purpose

Using up-to-date text and photographs is an excellent way to introduce a content-area (science, social studies, health) unit of study and to build background information about the topic.

Narrative

Holding up a copy of *National Geographic,* I say, "The article that I found so interesting is called 'Mending Broken Hearts.' It talks about how important it is to keep the heart healthy. And it explains what makes a heart sick or diseased. Scientists and doctors are making new discoveries about the heart every day—discoveries that they will pass on to us so that we can be smart about how we eat and live. We'll read a few paragraphs from the article in a minute. First, I want to share some photos with you."

I show the full-page color photo of a human heart en route to a heart transplant patient and say, "This photo shows the heart suspended in an experimental device that can keep it warm and beating much longer than the traditional way of immersing it in a saline solution and packing it in ice." "Ewww . . . " reacts Jen. "That's so gross!" "Not really, Jen," Anna counters. "I've seen pictures of the heart before and that's just what it looks like."

"Now, everybody, look carefully. What do you think the caption of this next photo might be?" "The heart!" several say in unison. "You're right," I say. "And just think, with today's technology, we're able to get a long, close look. This photo is a ten-second scan. No surgery. And the detailed pictures show doctors lots of things. Look closely, here. Do you see that narrowed artery? That's a potential danger spot." I turn several pages and stop at the picture of an angiogram. "See this arrow and what looks like branches? Well, the branches are arteries and the arrow points to a closed or blocked artery—not a good thing, as we'll find out." ◆

TIP Using strong visuals to teach content-area reading both motivates students and helps them retain new vocabulary; they attach memorable images to a new word. For more information and time-lapse photography of healthy and diseased hearts, see the following PBS and National Geographic Web sites: http//www.pbs.org/wgbb/nova/heart and ngm.com/0702

3 STEP THREE

Display on the overhead an excerpt from the article in which you've underlined eight to ten target vocabulary words. Read aloud and direct students to listen and follow along silently.

Purpose

Students hear new terms being read correctly and fluently. Students are able to relate the written form of the words with the pronunciation of words that they may have heard but not previously seen.

Narrative

I say, "Now I'm going to read parts from this article. Follow along as I read. Pay careful attention to the underlined words and phrases as I read them. I'll bet you have heard some of these terms on TV or listening to adults talk. After I finish reading, you'll get the chance to read and work together to learn the new vocabulary. Everybody ready?" Students listen as I read the excerpt. ◆

4 STEP FOUR

Work with students to help them determine big ideas in the excerpt and to pose questions. Encourage students to use the new vocabulary, even if they're not certain of the exact meaning.

Purpose

Continued teacher guidance at this stage supports students' understanding of new concepts and vocabulary.

Narrative

"So what is the author saying about hearts and heart disease? Let's list the big ideas." I put up a fresh piece of chart paper. Garrett offers, "Well, something called coronary heart disease is a big killer in the United States." "Okay. Good," I reply and write his idea on the chart paper. "What else?" "Cholesterol is bad for the heart," Jen says, "but I don't know why." "That's okay. We'll talk about it, Jen. I'll write down that cholesterol can prevent a heart from staying healthy. What else?" Sean says, "Doctors can give people with cholesterol something called a statin. I think that helps stop the cholesterol danger to the heart."

Other students volunteer ideas. The students' list of key ideas includes:

Too much cholesterol is bad for the heart.

Doctors prescribe medicines called statins to help lower cholesterol.

Modern cameras can take pictures of the heart with no surgery necessary.

A blocked artery is dangerous and can stop blood from flowing and the heart from pumping.

Medicine has a better way to keep a heart outside its body beating and pumping.

"Not bad! This article talks about lots of new ideas that may be unfamiliar to you. So, excellent first try at understanding!" ◆

5 STEP FIVE

Show the overhead transparency with a list of high-context sentences featuring the target vocabulary words. Invite volunteers to read the sentences aloud.

Purpose

Reading restated ideas from a text helps to confirm students' initial understanding of new concepts. Additional encounters with words in context provide further support in learning new vocabulary.

Narrative

Directing their attention to the overhead, I say, "Let's read some sentences that I wrote. I took some big ideas and new vocabulary and kind of summarized the excerpt that you read from 'Mending Broken Hearts.' Any volunteers?" Different students read the sentences. "Good job!" I comment. ◆

EXCERPTED SENTENCES WITH HIGHLIGHTED VOCABULARY

<u>Coronary heart disease</u> is the number one killer in the United States.

It can cause <u>heart attacks</u> and stop the heart from beating.

Blood flows from the heart through large <u>arteries</u>.

Where an artery bends, sticky, waxy <u>cholesterol</u> can form.

Most heart attacks are caused by <u>plaque</u> within an artery wall.

If <u>plaque</u> in an artery wall ruptures, a blood <u>clot</u> can form.

A <u>clot</u> can stop blood from getting to the heart muscle and the heart pump stops.

<u>Cardiologists</u> can prescribe <u>statins</u> to lower cholesterol formations in arteries. Doctors think that lowering cholesterol decreases the possibility of coronary heart disease.

6 STEP SIX

Students work in groups of four to create their own definitions for the new vocabulary words.

Purpose

Working with peers invites collaboration, and thus talk, about words. It also encourages students to engage with and explore new concepts.

Narrative

"Now I want us to focus on the new vocabulary words and see if we can define them. Try to come up with a definition by yourselves. Use the clues from the surrounding words to help you. I'll leave the sentences up on the overhead. There are eight vocabulary words and terms: *coronary heart disease, heart attacks, arteries, cholesterol, plaque, clot, cardiologist,* and *statin.* I'll give you an index card to use for each word. Write the word at the top of the card. Then write your definition under it."

I circulate around the room as groups work, offering assistance when needed. I hear lively conversations as students argue about and negotiate different words' meanings. "A statin is a pill, I think," offers Jill. "No, no. It's just a kind of drug that fights cholesterol. Where does it say it's a pill?" argues Josh. "I don't know," admits Jill, "just a guess." I interrupt, "Keep thinking, you guys. You're coming up with some good possible definitions." ◆

7 STEP SEVEN

Students work in the same groups to find dictionary definitions of each word. They compare their group definition with a dictionary definition.

Purpose

Students have an opportunity to evaluate their own definitions and to use what they have learned to select the right definition from those that appear in the dictionary.

Narrative

"Now we're going to consult our dictionaries to find meanings that support our group definitions. Or maybe the dictionary will say something entirely different. If that happens, you should go back to the sentence and rethink what the new word might mean. You might even have to change your group's definition. The dictionary definition that you choose should be similar to yours."

Josh asks, "But what if our definition is all wrong? Or we're really stuck?" I smile. "Don't worry, Josh. This isn't a test! We're simply playing with new words, trying to be a kind of word detective. The harder part is coming up with our own meanings. Then the dictionary should help you make that meaning better, kind of refine it. Okay? And I'll be around to help any group who's really stuck!"

As the groups work, I circulate. Again, I hear lively conversations and notice that most students seem to be enjoying the activity. "This is actually fun," says Deanna to her group. "Last year all we did was look up definitions and write in vocabulary notebooks. I don't think I ever really learned the words." "Me neither," agrees Josh. ◆

8 STEP EIGHT

The groups share their definitions for the new vocabulary words. Facilitate group discussion and help students create a class definition for each word.

Purpose

Students move from small-group interaction on word meaning to whole-class discussion. Repeated work with new vocabulary makes the words more familiar and helps students to develop instant recognition, or automaticity, upon encountering these words in their reading.

Narrative

"Okay, everyone," I begin. "Choose a spokesperson for each group to read your definitions. We'll work together to select a class definition for each term. Let's begin with *coronary heart disease*. Volunteers?"

Jen announces, "We'll go. Our definition says: *A disease that affects the heart.* Then we looked it up and found out that it's a condition that reduces blood flow through the coronary arteries to the heart. So we put the two together and came up with our new definition: *Coronary heart disease is a disease of the arteries to the heart that reduces blood flow and can cause heart problems.*" "Great job, group one."

I choose another group. "What did you guys write?" I ask. Garrett responds, "Well we sorta had some different ideas. At first we said *coronary* has to do with a crown or something. Anna said coronation and kings and stuff so we tried to figure out the word that way. When we looked it up in the dictionary, one definition did say, *resembling a crown or circlet.* So we were like, 'Yeah!' Then we figured it was a medical term that has to do with the veins and arteries that circle the heart. Our final definition is: *Coronary heart disease has to do with a problem in the veins or arteries surrounding and leading to the heart.*" I comment, "Wow, you guys are really thinking today! Another good definition. We have two more groups, so let's listen. Then we'll choose a class definition."

Group three's final definition reads: *Coronary heart disease slows down blood flow to the heart and it can cause a heart attack.* And the fourth group defines *coronary heart disease* as: *a condition of the heart's arteries that slows blood movement to the heart and can cause damage.* "Excellent work, everyone," I say. "We have four possible definitions. Which one do you think best defines *coronary heart disease*? Anna's hand shoots up. "Well, I like all of them but I think group one has the best because it tells where exactly the disease is and what exactly happens."

Heads nod. "Everyone agree?" I ask. "Yep!" responds the class. "Okay, then, we have a definition! I'll write it on a card and put it underneath the word card. I'll post both on our new word wizard wall."

We then proceed to the next vocabulary term and continue until the class has defined all eight. ◆

STEP NINE
Explain the procedure for the word wizard wall.

Purpose
Students can use the word wizard wall to showcase their word learning.

Narrative
I ask students to come sit in front of the word wizard wall. "You have all done a great job figuring out some tough new words. We'll be reading those words and other vocabulary terms as we study about the heart and the circulatory system. You can use this word wizard wall to help you remember and use the new words you have just learned. Here's how it works. Every time you use one of these words, take a wizard hat from the envelope on the board. Write your name on the hat and put it underneath the vocabulary term that you used. But before you can do that, you have to bring me evidence that you've used the word correctly. For example, if you're talking to your mom or dad about what we're studying in science, you might say: *Dad, did you know that statins are drugs that can lower high cholesterol?* To get credit, you'll have to tell me or your teacher exactly what you said. We decide if you have used the new vocabulary correctly. In the case of that sample sentence, you would get credit for *two* vocabulary words, right? *Statins* and *cholesterol*. You can also use the new words in your writing, either at school or at home. Just bring us evidence that you have used the word. At the end of our heart science unit, we'll count up who has the most wizard hats. That person becomes the grand wizard. You can also become a word wizard if you use a particular vocabulary term more than anyone else. Any questions?"

"Well, it sure will help us learn new words," offers Anna. "My mom says if I can use a word in a sentence and it makes sense, then I know it." "She's exactly right," I agree. "And if we *know* the words, we can read them instantly," I continue. "So . . . everyone see how learning and practicing new vocabulary can also make you better, fluent readers?" Heads nod. "Excellent!" ◆

CHAPTER FOUR

Reading With Appropriate Phrasing

Parents, teachers, and students applaud and Kathy Carhart's fifth graders beam. The class exhibition, the culminating event of a two-month genre study of provocative texts and social issues, is over. As their audience leaves, the fifth graders cluster around their poster displays in the school cafeteria. "Wow, all that hard work really paid off!" says Deanna. Others nod. "Yeah," agrees Peter, "it was easy to talk about our posters, but I never thought we'd be able to speak and perform our poems like that. Hey, Dr. M., guess that's why we practiced, huh?" "Indeed it was, Peter." I smile. "Indeed it was."

PORTRAIT OF A CLASSROOM WHERE STUDENTS MAKE LANGUAGE SING

Back in the classroom, students chatter excitedly, reluctant to return to the daily routine. Kathy quiets the room. Then she asks, "So . . . who wants to tell us how the exhibition this morning made you feel?"

Destinee's hand shoots up. "Ok, Destinee, go ahead!"

"Well, I was so scared at first. People were staring at me and I felt like I couldn't speak. But then I started, and the words just fell out. I mean, I really knew my poem. My mom said it showed 'cause I recited it so well. And Jamie's grandmother said my poem brought tears to her eyes—"

Elizabeth interjects, "My mom said the same thing! When she heard me read the words of my grandfather—her father—about World War II and the sadness and death, she said my poem brought back memories of stories she heard as a little girl—"

"The same happened to me," Peter and Neil say. And Brittany and Sarah add their: "Awesome! Exciting! It felt good! Can we do another exhibition, Mrs. Carhart?"

Kathy shakes her head and grins. "We'll see . . . we'll see. But, for now, is there anyone else who has something to say about today?"

Zach, who has been uncharacteristically quiet, slowly stands up and announces proudly, "Well, we have a surprise for you and Dr. M. We just decided to do this yesterday so we couldn't perform it at the exhibition. We worked on it after school. Can we show you now?"

"Absolutely!" we reply.

Zach walks to the front of the room and signals to Kyle, Andy, and Sean who gather around him, carrying bongo drums, sticks, and blocks. "We've put my poem to music," says Zach. "It's still a little rough, but here goes. Ready, guys?" Zach begins to read, accompanied by drum and percussion sound effects.

Different

I ride in the car
Bumping,
Thumping
Against my wheelchair.
We are going to the store . . .
Why is something so simple so complicated?

As we roam around searching for a parking spot,
I see that the handicapped spots are taken,

Taken by people who don't need them.
That hurts me.

People take our spots.
Do they know how hard it is for us?
I do not ask for sympathy,
I just ask for respect.

Then a wandering boy sees me.
He shouts, "Look at the handicapped boy."
It makes me feel worthless.

The manager is coming,
My mind is racing,
He explains to me,
"We don't allow handicaps to slow down the line."

So we leave.
Discrimination and hatred won.
I never wanted to be different.

Zach repeats, "I never wanted to be . . . different." And the beat of the
drum and wood blocks echo *dif-fer-ent, dif-fer-ent*. Zach and his musicians
bow, and the class applauds. "Wow! Excellent!" Kathy exclaims. "What a wonderful surprise. But, even more, how much you have learned about performing
poetry. I am so proud of you!"

At William Winchester Elementary School in Westminster, Maryland, classes often
stage schoolwide exhibitions. This particular morning represents the first exhibition of a new school year and it is a powerful showcase of what students learned
about important issues in today's world.

These fifth graders have read novels such as Karen Hesse's *Out of the Dust*
and Jerry Spinelli's *Maniac Magee*, which address poverty, homelessness, street vio-
lence, and discrimination. They have researched topics of their own choosing,

investigating gangs, talking to volunteers in soup kitchens, and listening to stories of adopted children and their parents.

The students have also listened to Gary Paulsen's novels, *NightJohn* and *Sarny*, and Walter Dean Myers' narrative poem "Locomotion," learning from these texts about telling a story and crafting beautiful writing. Ultimately, it is the students themselves who played key roles in planning the exhibition, electing to create trifold posters that display important facts about a self-selected social issue and agreeing to perform original narrative poems written about their topics.

But most important, as shown in the opening portrait, Zach and his peers understand that they must do more than merely recite facts and read poems. They know that memorable presentations engage an audience and this is what they strive to do. They *perform* their work, they make language *sing*, and their messages about poverty, homelessness, war, and discrimination resonate with all their listeners, young and old. These fifth graders' reading performances represent fluency at its best and reiterate the power of the spoken word.

THE IMPORTANCE OF READING WITH EXPRESSION

When a child is in the early stages of learning to read, we teachers focus on the word—"What are the sounds in that word?" "Look at that word and tell me what it is." "Let's use our word wall today." And so on. So we keep the syntax, or word order, of the sentence simple and gradually introduce the idea of fluent reading. "Read that the way you would say it," we prompt. But older readers, like Kathy's students, encounter complex sentences in their reading, like Jerry Spinelli's:

> Day after day, a mob of kids sat on the Beswick living room rug after school, goggled eyed and gaping like so many guppies at Willie the Worm on the ten-inch black and white screen floor.

The syntax of a sentence like that goes beyond the simple sentences in primary level reading. So, to build proficiency in reading, we introduce students to more complex syntax that, although not usually used in speech, is common in print. Authors "adorn" a simple sentence with phrases and clauses. The order "subject-verb-object" (*We had fun!*) is sometimes reversed to "object-subject-verb" (*What fun we had!*). Sentences grow in length. Signposts appear: commas, semicolons, italicized words, quotation marks. Phrasing becomes critical for fluency, as well as for meaning.

For many students, observing the way we model fluent reading of complex sentences is sufficient. As they practiced, Kathy's students studied the syntax of the texts they read and experimented with ways to make sense of lengthy sentences: pausing appropriately, grouping words together, monitoring for meaning as they read. Some students, however, often get lost in the maze of a complex sentence. Such readers need more structured support to read these longer, more complex sentences fluently. Our lessons need to hold these students' attention while we provide repeated practice with phrasing, and attending to those signposts.

Think for a moment about phrases. The most common are prepositional phrases, such as *in the house, on the table*, and *around the corner*. We find such phrases often in speech as well as in print. Some modify a noun: *the book on the table*. Some modify a verb: *ran around the corner*. Participle phrases (the *–ing* form of a verb) are less common in speech. When they describe a noun, they act as adjectives: *Running across the lawn, Chris tripped and fell*. For meaning, the reader needs to group the words in the phrase together. The comma signifies a pause. Our reader then needs to connect *running across the lawn* to *Chris*, i.e., what Chris was doing when he tripped and fell. Sometimes an *–ing* phrase can be used as a noun: *Running a 10-k race demands practice*. That requires grouping the words appropriately as well.

Readers also come across long sentences that combine clauses. Each clause could stand alone as a separate sentence, but the writer has chosen to combine them. Consider this example:

Mary ran ahead while her sister stopped to pick flowers.

Mary ran ahead has all the requirements of a complete sentence, as does *her sister stopped to pick flowers*. Joining these two clauses with the word *while* connects the two actions, adding a subtle meaning to the text—a meaning the reader should not overlook. There are several resources available to help you review grammar rules and find useful examples of signposts that fluent readers observe. Although some pertain to writing, these sources are also helpful in teaching students to become fluent readers. Marvin Terban's *Checking Your Grammar and Getting it Right* (1993), Constance Hale's *Sin and Syntax* (1999), and Constance Weaver's *Teaching Grammar in Context* (1996) are just three examples of such texts.

The lessons in this chapter provide students with practice in grouping words into

Clipping words to create a found poem (Lesson 2).

phrases to read complex sentences effectively. We have chosen to use poetry in several of the lessons because lines of poetry are often written—and read as—phrases in themselves. We also included choral reading, a supportive and engaging fluency activity that gives all readers a chance to participate—fluent readers can be paired with their less fluent classmates. The lesson on creating an i-movie brings home to students the role punctuation plays in fluent reading.

LESSONS IN THIS CHAPTER

Lesson One:

Chunking Words to Improve Fluency (page 83)

Objective: Practice fluent reading of phrases with guided instruction using a text segmented into phrases.

Lesson Two:

Found Poems: Phrasing Effectively by Tuning in to Print Cues (page 91)

Objective: Construct a poem using phrases found in print materials and practice reading the poem with proper phrasing and expression.

Lesson Three:

Newscast-Quality Readings With Student-Created iMovies (page 97)

Objective: Practice and perform student-written newscasts to deliver content-area information in an engaging, fluent way.

Lesson Four:

Choral Reading (page 104)

Objective: Attending to text cues like punctuation and to character development cues, practice and perform with peers one part of a two-character dialogue.

Lesson 1

Chunking Words to Improve Fluency

Taught by Catherine Hatch
Home-schooled student, Seattle, Wash.

INTRODUCTION

Older students whose oral reading lacks fluency sometimes hang onto the word-by-word habits they have built up over the years. Good readers parse, or chunk, groups of words into phrases, applying to words in print the syntactic features of the language they have learned through speech. Research on struggling readers suggests that word-by-word reading tends to interfere with comprehension. In fact, O'Shea, Sindelar, and O'Shea (1985) concluded that segmenting sentences into meaningful phrase units helps below-average students with comprehension. In other words, providing practice in chunking text is likely to improve comprehension for nonfluent readers. The authors suggest that text can be segmented into phrases by inserting spaces or vertical lines, underlining, or highlighting.

Since Nate, a home-schooled student whom we met in earlier lessons, is a word-by-word reader, Jane and her sister Catherine gave him practice in such chunking. This lesson describes the procedure they followed. It can also be used in the classroom with individual students. At the end of the lesson, we suggest ways to use practice in chunking with small groups of students.

PREPARATION AND MATERIALS NEEDED

- Copies of selected text, at or slightly above students' instructional reading level, segmented into meaningful phrases. (An excerpt from "The Aurora Borealis" by Jane Sullivan is used in this lesson.)

PROCEDURE, PURPOSE, AND NARRATIVE

1 STEP ONE

Introduce the purpose of the lesson: to read a selection that has been segmented into phrases.

Purpose

Beginning the lesson by setting goals helps the students focus on the task of making their reading aloud meaningful.

Narrative

"Nate, we're going to have some fun today," says Cathy. "Have you ever heard of the northern lights?"
"Yeah," Nate answers. "Joey and Michael saw them once when they

were in Canada." Cathy nods. "I remember that. Well, today, you and I are going to read a story about the northern lights." ◆

"Aurora Borealis" Excerpt, Segmented for Phrasing

It's winter / in Alaska. / Midnight. / Nine degrees above zero. / And yet / there are people, / grown-ups / bundled against the cold, / children / clothed in scarfs, gloves and fur-lined boots / outside, / looking at the sky. / Why? / It is because the sky / is putting on a show / for them, / a show / we call / the northern lights. / Scientists / call it / the aurora borealis. / Sometimes, / the northern lights / are soft clouds of white. / Sometimes / they dance / across the sky / in streaks / of blue and green, / yellow and red. / What causes / the northern lights? / Why can they be seen / only at night? / And why do they change / from night to night? / Scientists / have given us / some answers.

(Note: While we used slashes to segment the phrases, underlining, vertical lines, and highlighting are other options.)

---

2 STEP TWO

Introduce each new vocabulary word in the context of a sentence. When necessary, assist the student with pronunciation and/or meaning.

Note: It is helpful to make a list of the selected words and write a high-context sentence to reinforce the meanings of the words for the student (see page 85).

Purpose

Familiarizing the student with the meaning of words beforehand helps the student avoid hesitations and concentrate on the task at hand: chunking words meaningfully.

Narrative

Cathy puts a list of words on the table. "These are some words I think we should go over before we start to read. Let's see how many you know." She points to the word *degrees*. Nate looks at the word, squints a bit, and then says, *de . . . grees*. "And can you read that sentence?" Cathy asks. Nate nods. "*It is cold today. The temperature is thirty degrees.*" Cathy smiles. "Right. Now, here are some more words. They may be new to you. Let's go over them and see how many you know. I'll read the word. Then I'll read the sentence. Then you read it. Then, see if you can tell me what the word means."

Bundle—It is cold. We need to bundle up to stay warm.

"Wrap around you," says Nate.

Aurora borealis—Another name for aurora borealis is northern lights. "The sentence tells you," says Nate. "Aurora borealis *are* the northern lights!"

Aurora australis—Another name for aurora australis is southern lights.

"Same thing, says Nate. But this time he stumbles on the pronunciation. "The au-au-strail-is are by the South Pole." Cathy repeats the word again: "*Australis*" and has Nate pronounce it several times.

Particles—There are particles of paper on the floor. Nate defines that word without difficulty. "Pieces," he responds. Cathy continues in this same mode for the rest of the words she has identified as "new vocabulary" for Nate: *electron, solar, magnet, sphere, magnetosphere, nitrogen, oxygen, shimmering, arc, climate.* He does better as the lesson progresses but continues to stumble on troublesome words: *Australis, magnetosphere, nitrogen,* and *shimmering.* ◆

WORD LIST WITH SENTENCES IN CONTEXT FOR THE READER

Degrees	It is cold today. The temperature is 30 degrees.
Bundle	It is cold. We need to bundle up to stay warm.
Aurora borealis	Another name for aurora borealis is northern lights.
Aurora australis	Another name for aurora australis is southern lights.
Particles	There are particles of paper on the floor.
Electron	An electron is a particle with a negative charge of electricity.
Solar	We get solar energy from the sun.
Magnet	A magnet can pick up metal.
Sphere	A ball is shaped like a sphere.
Magnetosphere	The magnetosphere is one of the layers of gas around the earth.
Nitrogen	Nitrogen is a gas.
Oxygen	Oxygen is another gas.

3 STEP THREE

Give the student the text, separated into meaningful chunks as in the example above. Begin reading the story in phrases, sentence by sentence. Then have the student repeat the process. Continue until the student has demonstrated that he/she understands the procedure.

Purpose

Modeling the process shows the student what is expected of him.

Narrative

"I think we're ready to read this story," Cathy says. Here is your copy. You can see it looks a little strange. That's because, instead of writing the story in sentences, I put slashes between groups of words to make our story sound right. We'll read this story together. I'll read the phrases in each sentence first to show you what I want you to do. Then, you'll read them to me." Cathy reads, "*It's winter*," then pauses briefly, and continues: "*in Alaska.*" "Now, you read it." Nate reads: "*It's winter*," then pauses before continuing, "*in Alaska.*" "Good," says Cathy. "That's exactly how I want you to read the sentence. We call it 'chunking' when you do that." ◆

4 STEP FOUR

Continue modeling for the first two paragraphs or until it appears that the student can proceed on his own.

Purpose

Providing support for the student gives him confidence so that he can read the article independently. The repeated modeling reinforces the concept that we chunk words into meaningful phrases.

Narrative

"Let's read a few more sentences so you understand chunking. I'll read first, then you read," says Cathy, She reads the next several phrases, pausing at each slash: "*Midnight. / Nine degrees above zero.*" Then she looks up at Nate. "Now you try it," she says. "*Midnight . . . Nine . . . degrees . . . above . . . zero,*" he reads. "No," says Cathy. "Read the words as though you are saying them to me."

She rereads the phrases. This time Nate discards his word-by-word habit and chunks the words into phrases, reading with the fluency Cathy is looking for. She continues, "*And yet / there are people, / grown-ups / bundled against the cold,*" Nate follows her example, this time reading fluently, imitating the expression Cathy uses. Cathy nods and reads: "*children / clothed in scarfs, gloves, and fur-lined boots / outside, / looking at the sky.*" She looks at Nate. "So many clothes—they tell you how cold it is. Do you hear how my voice makes those words sound important? Listen. I'll read it again."

Nate listens, then imitates Cathy, emphasizing the same words. Satisfied that he understands, Cathy continues reading the paragraph, three or four chunks at a time. When it is his turn, she reminds him to read in a fluent, natural voice, as though he were talking. The two continue to the end of the paragraph. ◆

5 STEP FIVE

Ask the student what he remembers from the paragraphs you just read together. Provide prompts to see if he can recall any major facts omitted in the retelling.

Purpose

Asking a student to retell what he's read in his own words is a reliable strategy for checking comprehension—a key indicator of fluency.

Narrative

At the end of the second paragraph, Cathy pauses. "Let's stop here, and talk about what we've read," she says. "Tell me in your own words what you remember." Nate thinks, then says, "It's wintertime in Alaska and people are outside watching the northern lights. The people enjoy it because they put on a light show for them." Cathy prompts Nate for further information until she's satisfied that his comprehension is satisfactory. "Now," she says, "we'll read two more paragraphs, and then we'll stop and you can tell me what we read again." The two continue this routine for the next two paragraphs. ◆

6 STEP SIX

After the student has imitated your fluent reading satisfactorily, invite him to continue, but this time you'll whisper-read along with him. (You read together—as you read softly, or "whisper-read," the student reads the same words aloud.) Whisper-read the next two paragraphs in phrases.

Purpose

Whisper-reading continues to provide needed support but allows the student to take the lead in practicing the characteristics of fluent reading.

Narrative

"This time," Cathy explains, "I'd like to whisper-read with you. We'll read the next two paragraphs together. I'll read phrase-by-phrase and I want you to do that, too—but *with* me, not after me. And don't forget. Make it sound as though you were talking to me." Together, they read the next two paragraphs, with Cathy in the background and Nate accepting more responsibility for reading the phrases with the natural expression we find in fluent speech. ◆

7 STEP SEVEN

Pause at the next break point and ask the student to retell. Provide prompts to see if he can recall any of the major facts he has omitted.

Purpose

Continue checking comprehension as the student uses the fluency-building technique.

Narrative

After two paragraphs, Cathy calls a halt to the whisper-reading. "Okay," she says. "Let's stop here and talk about what you've read." Nate responds to her satisfaction. ◆

8 STEP EIGHT

As a trial, have the student read the next paragraph aloud by himself.

Purpose

It is important to see whether the student will continue to chunk words into phrases or resort to word-by-word reading when reading on his own.

Narrative

"You're doing a good job. I'd like you to read this next paragraph on your own. Remember, I still want you to read in phrases." Nate takes a breath but is stumped by the first word: *Imagine.*

Cathy waits a few seconds, then pronounces it for him. The word *huge* is his next problem. Once again, Cathy supplies the pronunciation.

"Let me start over," Nate says. He takes a running start and with the expression of an actor immersed in his role, reads the phrases, pausing at each break: "*Imagine . . . such huge lights . . . hanging high in space . . . one hundred miles high.*" Because Cathy has covered other difficult words (*electric, magnetosphere, nitrogen, oxygen*) in the vocabulary part of the lesson, they do not pose a problem: Nate reads the rest of the paragraph with a confidence he lacked at the beginning of this lesson. ◆

TIP To avoid hesitations over words, ask the student to scan the section you want him or her to read to look for "new" words—words that are unfamiliar in print. Pronounce those words for the student before the reading begins.

9 STEP NINE

Ask the student to retell that portion of the text. Provide prompts to see if he can recall any of the major facts he has omitted.

Purpose

Checking comprehension prompts the student to focus on the meaning of the passage.

Narrative

"Now, tell me what you learned from this part," says Cathy. "Well," Nate starts, then pauses to think. "They're like neon lights and they glow for hundreds of miles. And they're colored, like green and blue." ◆

10 STEP TEN

If the student did not read the previous paragraph satisfactorily, return to whisper-reading the next paragraphs. Otherwise, ask the student which he prefers: reading on his own or whisper-reading the rest of the passage. Honor his preference.

Purpose

Teachers should cease this support when a student's comprehension is high and he knows at least 95 percent of the words on sight. Students benefit from experiencing success, particularly in areas where failure has become routine.

Narrative

"Let's finish the article now," says Cathy. "Which would you rather do, read it on your own or whisper-read with me?" "I can read it by myself," Nate says confidently. "Okay," says Cathy. He reads the first few sentences in phrases but then loses the rhythm. He pauses on *curtains*, but decodes it correctly, using the context. Later, he mispronounces *our* as *or* and *sights* as *signs* but self-corrects. When he stumbles on *Exploratorium*, Cathy waits, then pronounces it for

him after three seconds. Able to recognize more words, he tries the section again, maintaining more successful phrasing. ◆

11 STEP ELEVEN

Ask the student to retell what he's just read. Provide prompts to see if he can recall any of the major facts he has omitted.

Purpose

Checking comprehension at this point helps the student recognize that he may need to reread parts to understand the section.

Narrative

"Now tell me what you remember from that part." Nate responds appropriately, recalling the important facts. Cathy rounds out the lesson with praise for his work. "That was a pretty long article with lots of new information for you," she says. "I'm proud of you." ◆

ADJUSTING THE LESSON TO INCLUDE A GROUP OF STUDENTS

You can follow the same procedure with a small group of students reading at the same level. While each takes a turn reading aloud, the other students can read the text silently. Each student can work with the teacher in turn, first repeating, then whisper-reading. Like Nate, students may, at first, have difficulty reading in phrases. With the teacher's modeling, they should be able to fall into the routine. Some may resort to word analysis when they come to unfamiliar words. Don't let that happen, since you are concentrating on fluency. Provide the pronunciation of these words immediately and take note of them. You can incorporate them into a vocabulary lesson at another time.

Lesson Two

Found Poems: Phrasing Effectively by Tuning in to Print Cues

TAUGHT BY NORFA HERNANDEZ (WITH JANE SULLIVAN ASSISTING) IN HER
AFTERNOON READING CLASS
LA ESCUELA INTEGRADA DE LOS NIÑOS TRABAJADOROS
ANTIGUA, GUATEMALA

INTRODUCTION

This "found poem" lesson is an exercise that combines writing with reading. Using newspapers, students, in pairs or individually, look for and cut out words and phrases they can use to create a poem. The rule is that they must find them in printed material. They then paste the words and phrases together to form a poem. Because students rehearse reading aloud their own compositions, the technique is especially effective for providing practice in grouping and reading words in phrases.

At the Integrada School, where this lesson took place, Jane demonstrated how to create a found poem in one of a series of reading/writing workshops given for the faculty. Because she had used the technique with students in her class, they asked Norfa, the sixth-grade teacher, to teach a lesson on found poems to a group of fifth and sixth graders who were having difficulty reading fluently. This lesson was conducted in Spanish, the students' native language. Jane observed and later, using the video Midge took and her own notes, translated the lesson from Spanish to English. It is an example of how universal such reading lessons are. In any language, motivated students learn.

PREPARATION AND MATERIALS NEEDED

- Copies of print material (e.g., newspapers, magazines—the material might be at or slightly higher than students' reading level), at least one copy for each pair of students
- Scissors
- Paste
- Cardboard or large pieces of paper
- Example of a found poem

PROCEDURE, PURPOSE, AND NARRATIVE

1 STEP ONE

Explain the purpose of the lesson: to use words and phrases from the newspaper to create a poem.

Purpose

Explaining the goal of the lesson in the beginning gives students an idea of what will be expected of them.

Narrative

"Today, we are going to write a poem, using these newspapers that I have brought," Norfa explains to her group of ten students. She holds up newspapers she has brought in. ◆

2 STEP TWO

Show students examples of clippings of words and/or phrases you can use to create the poem.

Purpose

Demonstrating the process makes it clearer for students.

Narrative

"I'll cut out words and phrases from this newspaper," Norfa explains. "Then, I am going to show you how I can use these words to make a poem." She picks up a page from the newspaper on her desk and clips a phrase of three words from it. "*En mi casa (In my house)*—I like this phrase," she says. "I think that I want to put it into my poem." ◆

3 STEP THREE

Demonstrate creating a poem with the words you have selected. Remind students that the lines of a poem do not necessarily have to rhyme. The poem should, rather, create an image, a picture, or an idea that they like. Demonstrate how to read the phrases fluently.

Purpose

Explaining as you demonstrate answers "why" questions that students might have. Building in the importance of fluency as part of reciting the poem makes the reading-writing connection clear.

Narrative

"Do you see how I've cut these words so I can use them in my poem?" Norfa points out. "Now I am going to look for other words or phrases that go with my first phrase." Cesar's hand goes up. "Any words at all?" he asks. Norfa nods. "Any words that go together," she answers. "When I read my poem, I'll read these words together—not word by word, like *in . . . my . . . house*. I'll read them smoothly, as though I am talking to you: *in my house*. So find words that say something—it could be one word or a whole phrase. See?" She points to another phrase on the clipboard. "Here I have another phrase: *my friends*. That goes with *in my house*. Maybe I'll use that, too. Remember, a poem doesn't always have to rhyme. The phrases should make us think about a picture or an idea, though. My phrases tell you about my house and how my friends are welcome in my house." She picks up the paper where she has already pasted the words of a poem together. "Here is a poem I already finished," she says. "When you are finished, your poem will look like this. My poem is about my family. Listen how I read each phrase. " She reads the poem aloud.

En mi casa
Mamá and Papá
Mis amigos
Mi familia
El amor llena mi casa.

(In my house / Mamá and Papá / My friends / My family / Love fills my house.)

"Can you hear the rhythm in the words? You try it now, together." The students read Norfa's poem in unison, imitating her phrasing. "Excellent," she says. "That is how you will read your poems when you are finished." ◆

4 STEP FOUR

Let students pair off. Distribute the printed material (newspapers) to each group. Remind students to look for words and phrases they might use in their poems. Make sure they understand that they may only use words they find in print.

Purpose

Working together lets students share creative ideas with each other. Because students only use words they find in print, the task becomes an exercise in both reading and writing.

Narrative

"Now, it's your turn," Norfa tells her students. "Choose a partner. Find the words you like in the pages of these newspapers. Make sure you recognize those words. If you don't, we'll help you. Do you have any questions?"

Hugo's hand goes up. "If we cannot find the word we want, can we write it in?" he asks. "The answer is no. You must only use words from the newspaper or magazine—you need to find the word you want there. So, you need to read as well as write, don't you? Are there other questions?" Since there are none, she has students pair up and enlists help from some in passing out the paper, newspapers, glue, and scissors they will need to create their poems. ◆

5 STEP FIVE

Oversee students as they work, making suggestions and encouraging them to use the cutout words or phrases creatively.

Purpose

Throughout the reading and selecting process, the teacher can frequently check that students understand the meaning and pronunciation of the words they've selected so that they will be able to structure a meaningful poem and accurately read all the words.

Narrative

As students search for and clip the words and phrases for their poems, Norfa and I go from group to group, assisting where necessary. Once students have found a word or phrase, we check to be sure that the pair can identify the words on sight. ◆

6 STEP SIX

Model reading challenging phrases fluently for students who are having difficulty reading them. Provide the necessary practice until they can read the phrases fluently by themselves.

Purpose

Teachers provide individual assistance as needed.

Narrative

I stop at Hugo's desk. "Read this phrase for me," I ask him, pointing to *What is the dream*, the phrase he has just assembled. He reads it slowly—word by word, without expression.

I model for him. "That is such a beautiful phrase," I say. "What made you choose those words?" Hugo smiles. "I like to dream," he says. "Ah! I like to do that, too. Now, listen to the way I read it," I say, reading the words with the correct emphasis. "I am asking a question. Do you hear the question? Do you hear my voice go up?" Hugo nods. "You read it like that," I say.

He reads the words again, as I run my finger under them to guide his voice. I turn to his partner, Cesar, who has been listening. "Now, you do it, Cesar," I say. I read the phrase again. Cesar imitates my intonation. I praise the pair and move on to the next group. ◆

7 STEP SEVEN

Once the groups have created their poems, have each student read the poem aloud to his or her partner. Emphasize the importance of "smooth reading." Students should repeat reading the poem until they can read each line fluently.

Purpose

Practice is necessary if students are to read with fluency.

Narrative

"Now that you have all written your poems, I want you to practice reading them. Jane and I will come around and help you." I return to Hugo and Cesar. "Your poem is so beautiful," I tell them. "Tell me about it." Hugo responds. "It tells how important a dream is," he says. "And these?" I ask, pointing to the other lines. "A dream is inside you," Cesar explains. "What you hope will happen someday and how you need to work to make it come true."

I am impressed with these ideas from boys so young. "When you read your poem aloud, your voice needs to say all that," I explain. "It must tell the others about your dreams. Let's practice that now." I read the first line aloud and invite the two boys to read it with the same fluency:

¿Qué es el sueño de todos?
Las frases de mi corazón
Esta semana
Este espacio
Puede poner el color
en la vida
y los sueños
Y los esperos secretos

(What is the dream of everyone? / The phrases of your heart / This week / This space / Can put color / To life and dreams and secret hopes)

For each phrase, I say, "Listen to me read this phrase." Then I read it aloud, running my finger underneath the words. Hugo takes his turn and reads the phrase with expression, and I nod to Cesar. Cesar is not as fluent a reader. He reads each word as though it stands alone, not chunking the words into phrases. I coach him to use natural expression as he reads each phrase. "Look up at me," I encourage him, "and say that phrase."

Cesar says the phrase, this time without hesitation. "Now, read it like that," I say, pointing to the words. He reads the phrase again. With several repetitions, Cesar gains confidence and begins to chunk the words, reading each phrase more fluently. ◆

8 STEP EIGHT

Have the pairs prepare to read the poem to the class. They should decide on their own how that should be done—a shared reading, alternating lines, and so forth. They should highlight their respective lines to make reading easier. Encourage students to include actions or gestures with the reading if they choose.

Purpose

Ending with a final performance motivates students to practice reading and work on their fluency. Highlighting parts allows students to perform their parts more accurately. Actions add expression and make the performance more interesting for the audience.

Narrative

"Now we're going to prepare to read our poems to the class," Norfa says, and suggests that each pair find a way to present its poem that includes both readers. Cesar and Hugo decide to take turns reading each of the lines. To help each of them remember which lines he will read, I have them mark the lines in colors. I take a red marker. "You be red, Cesar," I say. "Put a red dot at the beginning of each line you will read, like this." Once Cesar has marked his lines, I turn to Hugo. "Here's a green marker for you," I say. "Now, you mark your lines green. The dots will tell you when to read."

The two boys hold up their poem poster and practice reading it. "Remember, you can use actions, too—like *frases de mi corazón* [phrases from my heart]," I say, reciting from their poem while putting my hands on my heart. The boys grin and imitate me. I know they'll do well, so I move on to another group. ◆

9 STEP NINE

Give each pair of students the opportunity to read its poem before the class.

Purpose

Such a performance gives students a goal: to share their writing.

Narrative

After Norfa has checked that each of the five groups has practiced its found poem satisfactorily, she announces. "Now, let's listen while each pair reads its found poem aloud. Remember, you can put drama and expression into your poems."

One by one, the groups bring the poem they have created to the front of the room and read in chorus. The others listen quietly, and at the end, show their appreciation with applause. I listen, in particular, to Hugo and Cesar. Our practice pays off as the two abandon their word-by-word habit and read with a fluency that was not there when we began working together. They glance at me as they finish, proud of their accomplishment. Once again, I am convinced of the importance of modeling coupled with repeated practice in teaching students to read fluently. ◆

Lesson Three

Newscast-Quality Reading With Student-Created iMovie

TAUGHT BY MIDGE MADDEN IN KATHY CARHART'S FIFTH-GRADE CLASS
WILLIAM WINCHESTER SCHOOL, WESTMINSTER, MD.

INTRODUCTION

Prosody, as discussed earlier in this chapter, describes the rhythmic and tonal aspects of spoken language (Hudson, Lane, & Pullen, 2005), features such as intonation and stress patterns, which are at the heart of expressive reading (Allington & Cunningham, 1983; Dowhower, 1991). The reader who reads with natural expression or prosody *sounds* like he or she knows the meaning of the text, often using cues from the text (Schreiber, 1980). In fact, research suggests a reciprocal relationship between prosody and reading comprehension (Kuhn & Stahl, 2000)—a reader who can use tone and emphasis to read expressively most likely understands what the text means. It is possible, as we mentioned earlier, for a fluent reader to focus so much on natural expression that he or she fails to attend to the meaning embedded in the words. This is why it is important to check the reader's comprehension before drawing that conclusion.

This lesson focuses on developing readers who read with expression, or with prosody. We use student-created texts because readers struggle less with meaning when they've actually produced the text. Consequently, they can focus on reading with appropriate expression. We also believe that having autonomy over a text engages students in ways that practicing teacher-selected passages does not; students more readily *choose* to work on developing fluency.

We find that iMovies offer an excellent opportunity to foster both student writing and prosodic reading. They also tap into students' fascination with computers and technology, providing additional motivation. (We use Apple's software because it's easy to use. Movie software for Windows PCs can also be used, but it requires more experience with computers.)

The following lesson describes one part of creating an iMovie. In this particular example, the iMovie, *The Impact of Sports on Today's Society,* is the culmination of a fifth-grade sports genre study. It includes videotaped interviews, sports clips, and downloaded photos.

To prepare for the iMovie production, students first practice reading a piece of original writing (in the case of this lesson, a feature article on a sports topic). They attend closely to reading with smoothness, expression, and appropriate inflection. Then they record their performance using the computer's camera and microphone. In fact, with iMovie's captioning function, students can input the text beforehand and then read it as it scrolls across the screen, much as a news anchor would. Allowing students to "perform-read" their writing moves school assignments to a more authentic level. Students understand that their writing will have a wider audience and purpose when it appears in an iMovie documentary—and a more interested audience when they deliver information in an engaging, fluent way.

PREPARATION AND MATERIALS NEEDED

- Mac computer with iMovie software and built-in camera
- Microphone, either external or built into the computer
- Two copies of feature articles students have written during the unit

PROCEDURE, PURPOSE, AND NARRATIVE

1 STEP ONE

Students participate in a class meeting to brainstorm possibilities for an iMovie. The iMovie will showcase student learning across a four-week genre study.

Purpose

Taking ownership over their work increases students' enthusiasm and engagement in the project.

Narrative

"We're finishing up our sports study, and I need you guys to help me plan a way to celebrate our learning!" I continue, "Mrs. Carhart and I thought you might enjoy making an iMovie but we need your ideas."

"Cool!" respond Neil and Tyler. "We could talk about our questions and maybe—" "Yeah," interrupts Andrew, "and maybe read parts of our feature articles." "Good," I agree. "So if one part of our iMovie will be us reading parts of our feature articles, how do we go about doing it?" Deanna volunteers, "Well, we have to know our articles, first, of course. So, I guess we'll have to do some practice reading." "Okay, good start," I say. "What else?" Sean adds, "How 'bout we read to a partner? Then our partner can help us read really good. Maybe even suggest a best part to read for the iMovie."

"Great ideas!" I say. "Today, let's concentrate, then, on practicing and taping feature article excerpts for the iMovie. Later, we can add more to our movie, maybe even videotape our final sports debate. Remember the iMovie that I showed you about seeing-eye dogs? And we talked about how you produce it in parts?

Well, we can create our movie in parts, too. This reading of our feature articles can be the first piece. Everybody agree?" Heads nod and I continue, "Okay, great. But before we practice reading, let's think about what we do when we read with expression and the things our audience should listen for." ◆

2 STEP TWO

Students and teacher create a simple checklist for the characteristics of oral reading expression, or prosody. (See example below.)

Purpose

The checklist gives students a framework to use to evaluate their expression.

Narrative

"I'm going to chart some things for us to keep in mind when we listen to each other read our feature articles," I begin. "Raise your hand if you have any ideas."

Andy offers, "You have to watch punctuation at the end of the sentence, like change your voice and stuff if there's a question mark or an exclamation mark." "Okay, good," I nod. "We call that your tone of voice or inflection." I write: *Match tone of voice or inflection to the end punctuation in the text.* "What else?" I ask. "What about punctuation inside a sentence like commas or semicolons? They help us read in correct phrases," Sarah adds. "Another important thing," I reply, and write: *Use punctuation to pause at appropriate points in the text.*

"Well, my article has some quotes in it from famous sports players," Zach says. "Some players' words are funny but others are angry. So, don't I have to change the way my voice reads these quotes? I mean, sound funny or mad? Kinda like I'm acting?" "Excellent!" I say. "How about I put it this way?" I write: *Use appropriate tone of voice to represent characters' emotions, such as excitement, anger, or sadness.* "These are all important listening criteria for reading with expression. Is there anything else you can think of?" I pause, "Think of what a good read-aloud sounds like. In a way, your reading of your sports articles in our iMovie *is* a good read-aloud." Peter says, "Oh, I know! You have to know all the words—I mean no

---

HOW WE READ WITH EXPRESSION

- Match tone of voice or inflection to the end punctuation in the text.
- Use punctuation to pause at appropriate points in the text.
- Use appropriate tone of voice to represent characters' emotions, such as excitement, anger, or sadness.
- Know all the words and read smoothly.

stumbling—and you have to read real smooth." "Let's add your idea," I say, writing: *Know all the words and read smoothly.* "Good job, everyone," I say. "We'll title our chart "How We Read With Expression." You can use it to help you give feedback to your partner." ◆

3 STEP THREE

Students pair up and read their articles aloud to one another.

Purpose

Practicing helps students read their writing smoothly with expression.

Narrative

"Now, let's get our articles and pair up. Bring both copies of your article with you," I direct. Students find a partner and prepare to practice reading aloud. I encourage readers to

think about fluency and remind them to refer to the chart when they practice. "Remember," she encourages, "fluent readers make their audience *want* to listen. You are performing your work, so don't hold back! Let your voice change in pitch and volume and speak your words clearly and distinctly." ◆

4 STEP FOUR

Students give feedback to each other, following the guidelines on the chart.

Purpose

Receiving feedback helps readers perfect their oral reading performances.

Narrative

Kathy and I circulate while student pairs read to one another and critique one another. Andy and Zach huddle together at a desk. As Andy finishes reading, Zach offers, "I really like your article—you make a good point

about out-of-sight salaries. But you need to end it stronger, somehow. You know how our chart says 'match tone or voice to end punctuation'? Well, I think you should read it like you really mean that last line. You just kinda read it softly and stop."

Andy nods, "I get it, I think. Let me try again." He begins clearly and strongly, "I still wonder how it hasn't gotten through baseball's head that they need a salary cap." He pauses for an instant, then continues clearly and smoothly. "The NBA has one and the league is doing great. The NFL has a salary cap and the league is doing fantastic." Again, Andy pauses briefly, then finishes, becoming louder and more emphatic. "But baseball? Baseball doesn't have one and the league is heading for a strikeout!"

"Now, that's good!" says Zach. "Loud, clear, and you put lots of feeling in your voice!" ◆

5 STEP FIVE

Students identify the part of their feature articles they'll record.

Purpose

Giving students as much latitude as possible over the production keeps motivation high.

Narrative

"Okay, guys, we are hearing great expression in your reading. Now look over your feature articles again and pick one small part that you really like. It should be enough text to make sense. That's the piece you will read for the iMovie." Students silently reread their feature articles, selecting excerpts. ◆

6 STEP SIX

Student pairs practice reading their excerpts to one another. They critique one another's reading again, following the guidelines on the chart.

Purpose

To give fluent and prosodic reading performances, students must practice and integrate feedback.

Narrative

Again, we move around the room, listening to students as they help one another read with feeling and expression. We smile as we hear Kate really getting into her topic. Standing with one hand resting on her desk and the other holding out her text, Kate speaks with loud indignation: "Have you ever been to a baseball park right after the game? Just imagine . . . Spilled popcorn, lollipops stuck to the bleachers, soda-pop cans decorating the rows like tinsel on a tree!" Her voice rises, then stops. She continues, reading more slowly. "It's all trash, just left there and ignored." Kate pauses, then reads her last sentence, slowly and clearly articulating each word. She ends with a rise in volume and a strong emphasis on the final three words. "But not just leftover food and snacks claim the title 'trash' . . . *humans do too.*" ◆

7 STEP SEVEN

Students type their text into the iMovie software program. They can each determine the appearance and pacing of the words onscreen.

Purpose

Reading their text as it scrolls across the page enhances students' pacing and fluency. (The captions also help viewers develop their own fluency as they watch the iMovie and read the words that the speaker articulates.) Encouraging students to add punctuation, italics, and boldface to their writing makes it easier for them to read with appropriate pacing and emphasis.

Narrative

I compliment the students on their practice readings and give directions for the final taping. "Great job, everyone. Mrs. Carhart and I could really hear such wonderful expression in your voices as you read. Now we're going to begin taping each of you as you read your selected excerpt from your feature article." Zach interrupts, "Yikes, Dr. M., I'm really nervous. What if I mess up?" I smile. "That's OK, Zach. We can also retape. But remember, that's why we use punctuation, italics, and boldface in our writing. These are clues to help us read smoothly and with good expression."

"Okay," announces Kathy, "here's how it will work. We'll ask each of you to come back to the computer. Just bring your article excerpt. First, you will type in your words. Then we'll videotape you reading as the words move across the screen." ◆

8 STEP EIGHT

Students record their selected excerpts of their feature on the computer.

Purpose

Recording their writing for the public motivates students to become fluent, expressive readers.

Narrative

I caution the students that the taping takes time, and direct them to work quietly on other assignments as they wait for their turn. Brittany, the first to record, sits excitedly at the computer. She selects the font and types in her excerpt, adding punctuation and highlighting words for emphasis. She proofreads her work, then sets the speed at which the words will move across the screen. "I'm ready, Dr. M. Turn on the camera!"

Brittany reads the words as they scroll across the bottom of the page. The computer screen shows a transformed Brittany, composed and staring seriously at the camera as she reads: "In the 1800s, women were treated like pretty dolls by men. They were nothing—zip, zero—they simply didn't matter. They wore corsets that pulled their stomachs in and up to make them look pretty. These corsets also caused death, but men didn't care as long as their wives looked pretty. However, in 1892, women began to lose their doll image and were allowed to play basketball. Women have come a long way since then but aren't there yet. In 1989 an AFF study of television showed that 92 percent of televised sports are men's, 3 percent are women's, and 5 percent are neutral topics. Don't you think women deserve more respect than that? Jackie Mitchell, who struck out Babe Ruth, or Toni Stone, a baseball lover, is unknown to the 'normal' sports lover. Never heard of them? Well you just proved my point."

The class applauds. "Wow, you sounded like Barbara Walters!" exclaims Sean. "Can I go next?" I smile and nod. "Sure, Sean. You're on!" Student by student, the fifth graders record their writing, reading with expression and appropriate phrasing. ◆

Lesson 4

Choral Reading

TAUGHT BY JANE SULLIVAN IN DAVID JACKSON'S FIFTH-GRADE CLASS
UPPER TOWNSHIP ELEMENTARY SCHOOL, UPPER TOWNSHIP, N.J.

INTRODUCTION

Choral reading of text is an effective activity for improving fluency. The repeated oral readings give even the least fluent student practice in the instant word recognition, appropriate phrasing, and prosody that fluency requires. Fluent readers in the group provide the model, carrying those less fluent along in their chorus of voices. Poetry in particular lends itself to this activity. Short poems are easily repeated, and rhyming patterns help students with word recognition.

It is not difficult to find picture books that feature poems written as a dialogue between two characters. *Hey, Little Ant*, which we used in this lesson, is such a text. *Joyful Noise: Poems for Two Voices* is yet another. Margaret Wise Brown's *Runaway Bunny*, a non-rhyming text, is another example of a book that works well for choral reading. A word of caution, however. If we choose poetry, we need to model the proper prosody. We want our students to avoid the singsong rhythm they sometimes adopt when reciting simple rhymes.

PREPARATION AND MATERIALS NEEDED

- Chart listing characteristics of fluency (see page 23)
- Individual copies of a poetry text written as a dialogue between two characters

PROCEDURE, PURPOSE, AND NARRATIVE

1 STEP ONE

Remind students that in recent lessons you've talked about the importance of reading fluently. In today's lesson the class will learn how choral reading helps to develop fluency.

Purpose

Connecting today's lesson with previous lessons on fluency answers the common "why are we doing this?" question.

Narrative

"You've heard me use the word *fluency* quite a bit lately. You told me what we mean by 'reading fluently.' And we've done some exercises that help us become fluent readers. Today, we're going to do another exercise that helps us to practice reading fluently. We call it choral reading. Has anyone done choral reading before?"

Austin's hand goes up. "We did it in third grade," he informs the class. "Okay, so you already know something about this. Tell me how it works, Austin," I say. He hesitates, then begins, "Let's see. You all read a poem together." Rebecca chimes in, "And you read it in groups, like one side of the room starts and the other side reads the next line, and you go back and forth like that." "We did it in verses," says Hannah. "Each row took a verse." Austin picks up the thread: "And you all have to start together and read all the words together, like a chorus." "So, it's a bit like singing," I suggest. "Yeah, but you're saying the words, not singing them," Austin continues. "And you have to do those things that make it fluent," Steph offers. "Like say the words with expression and read them smoothly without stopping . . ." "Well, it sounds like you've done this before and you know what to do. So we can start," I say. ◆

2 STEP TWO
Review the features students previously identified as characteristic of fluent reading

Purpose
Such review serves as a reminder for students before they begin to read.

Narrative
"Let's first review what we know about fluency," I say to students, calling their attention to the chart. "*Automaticity*," I read, pointing to the first word on the chart. "Who can tell me what that means?"

Mia offers, "Knowing all the words without thinking about it?" The group accepts her answer, and we move on to the next feature, punctuation. This time Evan answers. "You notice the periods and commas: like you stop at periods, pause at commas." "Yes," I agree. "Punctuation marks are like traffic signs we see on the road. And you're right: we have to follow the directions that go with those signs. What about phrasing?" Hannah's hand goes up. "You need to read groups of words, like *down the road*—they belong together." "Thank you, Hannah," I say, nodding. "And now, here's that great new word." I point to the word *prosody*. Jeffrey speaks up. "That's reading as though you're talking."

"Good review, all of you. Now let's see if we can weave together all those elements in our group reading today." ◆

3 STEP THREE

Introduce the book you will use in the lesson and go over its layout.

Purpose

A quick walk-through of the text helps students visualize the story as a whole.

Narrative

I hold up a copy of *Hey, Little Ant* and begin with an introduction. "This is a great short story," I tell them. "I think it will lead to some interesting thoughts and discussions." I page through the book, showing the illustrations. "You can see from the pictures," I continue, "that there are only two characters in this story. And they are . . . " I pause for a response. Sarah is quick to answer. "A boy and . . . " she hesitates as she squints at the picture. "It looks like an ant." "An ant indeed," I respond. "So we know right away that this book will be which: nonfiction or fiction?" "Fiction," Derrick offers. "Ants can't have conversations with people." "And what else do we know through these pictures?" I ask, as I turn the page. Jeffrey makes a prediction, "It looks like the kid wants to kill the ant." Erica agrees. "And that's not right," she adds. ◆

4 STEP FOUR

The teacher and another fluent reader read the text while students listen.

Purpose

Showing is always a better approach than merely telling. Modeling allows students to observe the task being carried out, making it easier for them when it's their turn.

Narrative

"Now, Mr. Jackson and I are going to read the text aloud. He will read the part of the boy and I'll be the ant. What I'd like you to do is to listen to us as you look at the illustrations. So, I'll need two volunteers to hold up the book so everyone can see the pictures. Maybe a third person can turn the pages."

Hands go up and I choose Jessica, Rebecca, and Evan. David and I read through the book, careful to dramatize the scenes with vocal expression. ◆

5 STEP FIVE

Hold a brief discussion about the story with students.

Purpose

Since fluent reading is associated with comprehension, it is wise to check for understanding in lessons that emphasize fluent reading.

Narrative

"Let's talk about the story. Was it simply a conversation between a boy and a talking ant or was there a message buried in this story?" I ask.

Rebecca responds first. "It doesn't have an ending," she says. "You don't know if the boy kills the ant or not. You have to figure it out for yourself." "Yes," I answer. "The author invites us to decide what the last scene was. Why do you think he did that?" Evan speaks up, "He wanted us to put ourselves into the story?" I nod. "Good thinking, Evan. And how would you end it?" Evan continues, "I don't know. I guess I'd let him go. He's got a family to take care of."

The discussion continues. Satisfied that students have grasped the meaning of the story, I move to the focus of today's lesson: phrasing as a factor in fluency. ◆

6 STEP SIX

Have students critique the fluency the readers demonstrated in their performance, referring to the fluency characteristics chart as needed. If necessary, prompt them to see how the readers used these characteristics to bring out the story's message.

Purpose

Giving a critique requires students to consider the characteristics of fluency that will help them in their own performances.

Narrative

"Okay, you heard how Mr. Jackson and I read the story. Did we read fluently?" A chorus of yesses arises. "Thank-you," we say, each taking a modest bow. "But how do you know? What did you hear that makes you say yes?"

"You read with expression," Sarah calls out. "And, what did you hear, Sarah, that tells you that?" I ask. "You sounded scared," Sarah answers, "and you were pleading and Mr. Jackson sounded like a mean kid. "You didn't read too fast," Steph offers. "We could understand what you were saying." "It sounded like you were talking, not reading," Austin adds. I glance at the chart hanging on the front board, "Anything else?" Derrick raises his hand. "You put the words together, in phrases. You didn't stop without a warning," he says, glancing at the chart. "And you paid attention to punctuation," Mia adds, "Like when you asked a question."

"So, what you are telling me is that the way we read helped you understand the point of the story," I say. "And you are right. You need to do all these things when you read," I run my hand down the list of fluency features on the chart, "so that your listeners get the message. Can you do that?" Heads nod all around. "Then let's try it." ◆

7 STEP SEVEN

Divide the class into two groups and assign each group a part. Allow students to go over their lines before asking them to perform.

Purpose

After observing a model of fluent reading, students need an opportunity to imitate it.

Narrative

"First, let's divide the class the easy way. Boys on the left side, girls on the right," I say. Students scramble to get to the assigned side of the room.

"Okay, I am going to give each of you a copy of the text of *Hey, Little Ant*. You heard Mr. Jackson and me read the lines aloud. Now we want you to do the same thing, but in two groups. You'll choral-read the story. You can practice reading your lines together softly so you can get used to them. You need to listen to the rest of the group so you stay together, pause at the same places, and say some words softly and others louder. Once you're reading fluently as a group, we'll put our performance together."

David works with the boys' group and I take the girls. We caution them not to read in a singsong manner. "Make it sound as if you were talking instead of reading or chanting," we remind them. We go over the parts. "Okay," I say. "Let's look at the first page. What do you think the ant's voice should sound like?" Mia speaks up first. "She's scared so it needs to sound like that." "And she's so little, so it should be kind of squeaky," Jessica continues. "And pleading," adds Sarah. "So you need to say it softly?" I ask. "Yes, in the beginning," Hannah says. "But then, she needs to speak up. Like she's teaching the boy a lesson." "So, you'll gradually get louder as the ant gets bolder?" I ask.

We try out those suggestions. "Watch the punctuation," I remind them. I lead them as a conductor would so they phrase correctly and practice repeating the words together. After about ten minutes' practice, I call the class back together. ◆

8 STEP EIGHT

Have students read their part of the story in chorus several times.

Purpose

Practice helps students read fluently.

Narrative

I begin with an introduction: "A choral reading of *Hey, Little Ant* by Mr. Jackson's fifth-grade class." Then I nod to the boys. The two groups go through the text, the better readers carrying the less fluent ones along. We repeat the exercise several times. The reading grows smoother and more competent as the groups become more familiar with the text. We end the session with applause for both performances. ◆

CHORAL READING AS A TRANSITION ACTIVITY

Because students enjoy this activity so much, and readers benefit from repeated practice, this can be an activity you use anytime to pull the class together, for example, during a transition between classes or an unexpected wait for an assembly.

CHAPTER FIVE

Why and How We Assess Fluency

It is late summer and Janice Betts, a teacher and a colleague of ours, has recruited some young volunteers to meet with her and have a discussion about reading, fluency, and assessment.

PORTRAIT OF A GROUP OF STUDENTS DISCUSSING FLUENCY

"Let's sit out here on the porch for a while and have a little conversation," she says. The four youngsters, Felicia and Thaddeus, fourth graders, Hannah, a fifth grader, and Alex, a sixth grader, scramble for seats around the small table where Janice is sitting.

"We're going to talk about testing," she says. The students groan. "No, no," she continues quickly. "I'm not going to test you. I just want you to tell me how you feel about testing."

"Whe-e-w," says Felicia, wiping her brow. "I thought you were gonna give us a test." The others laugh and nod.

"Let's begin," says Janice. "I'm going to ask you some questions. Just chime in whenever you want. Okay?"

"Just say something and not raise our hands?" asks Alex.

"Right," answers Janice. "Just tell me your thoughts. First of all, suppose your teacher says to your class, 'Tomorrow, we're going to take a test in . . . some subject.' What's your reaction?"

"Please be science!" says Thaddeus.

"That's your favorite subject, Thad, isn't it? Who else? How would you react, Hannah?"

Hannah hesitates, then says, "Umm, study. I would study so I could get an A."

"What would you say, Alex?" Janice asks.

"I'd better get working?" he answers.

"So, I guess you all think you should study, right?" All four nod. "What would happen if you couldn't study for it, though?" she continues. "Something like—a test of how fast you can run. What would you do then?"

"I would just go and do it," replies Hannah.

Alex agrees. "I'd just start running."

"Me, too," Felicia chimes in.

Janice continues. "Let's see. You know when we say 'Eat your carrots' or 'Eat your broccoli' or whatever. They're good for you. Can we say anything like that about tests? Take this test; it's good for you? In other words, do you get anything out of taking tests?"

"You can't eat it," Felicia says, giggling.

"It can help you do better in college," Hannah adds.

"It helps you get better in the subject?" Alex offers.

Janice prods further, "What about you, Felicia, do you get anything out of taking a test?"

"Helps you learn . . . stuff that you don't know about," Felicia answers. "It helps you remember it?"

"So," Janice summarizes, "even though we might not like to take tests, there is some good to them, even when you can't prepare for some of them ahead of time, right?" They all nod.

"What about reading? How do tests in reading help you?"

Thaddeus speaks up this time. "They help you to read better?"

"How?" asks Janice.

"Because then you remember what the words are and so if you're reading a book and one of the words pops up that you had on the test, you'd be able to know it," Thaddeus says.

"Okay." Janice turns to Hannah. "What about you, Hannah? How does a reading test help you?"

"Well, it helps you remember the words and when you get older and there's a hard word, you'll know it because you saw it on a test," Hannah offers.

"Wait! I know. You read the same words over and over again and so you start to memorize them and you don't have to stop to think what they are," Alex says.

"Okay," nods Janice. "Now, I'm going to ask you a question. It's about a word that you might know. Do you know what I mean when I ask you: Do you read fluently?"

"Sometimes," answers Thaddeus.

"Do you know what that means?" Janice asks again.

"Doesn't that mean that when you're reading a book, you read it like it's happening in your life?" Thaddeus asks.

"Is it when you read it slowly and you're into the book and like you have your own ideas?" suggests Hannah.

"I think this may be a new word for you guys," Janice comments. Then she explains. "It's like reading with expression—reading as though you are actually talking, not reading word by word."

All the faces brighten and Alex adds, "I've had to read like that. We had a thing in social studies where you pick an explorer and you gotta write a whole story about it and then you had to get up in front of the class and read it out loud with expression, as though the explorer was telling it."

"So that would be reading what?" Janice prompts.

"Fluently?" Alex answers.

"Right. Like you were talking," Janice says. "Has anyone ever given you a test to see how fluently you read? Has any teacher ever asked you to read fluently? With expression?"

"Not for a test," Alex responds.

Felicia thinks a bit, then answers, "Well, the teachers would usually say, 'Read with expression,' if we were reading out loud."

"Have teachers ever asked the rest of you to read like that?"

"Only when you're reading out loud, they remind you," says Hannah. Thaddeus shakes his head in agreement.

"So, it's just a part of your reading groups," comments Janice, "but not taking you aside to see how well you can do it?"

They all shake their heads.

"Let's say I hand you a magazine you've never seen before," Janice begins. "I say to you: I want to see how fluently you can read. So, turn to page five and start reading that page aloud to me. How do you think you'd do?"

"I'd do really good," answers Alex confidently. The others nod.

"So, you might read it fluently . . . but some students wouldn't. What can a teacher do to teach them how?" Janice asks.

"Maybe, every time you read, your teacher could say, 'Read it with expression,' so you could get used to it," suggests Felicia.

"What if a teacher gave you a piece to read aloud and gave you 60 seconds. How would you feel about that?" Janice asks.

"Oh, no!" groans Alex. "I wouldn't like that. I would be pressured."

"And, you don't have time to read and think about what you read," adds Hannah. "It doesn't make any sense."

Janice thanks the students for their ideas and turns them loose to play together in her backyard. We talk about the views of testing and fluency that these middle-grade students have shared. And we agree. The words of Felicia, Thaddeus, Alex, and Hannah provide valuable insights into the ways that teachers need to think about testing, and particularly, the teaching and testing of fluency.

Why We Assess

Most students, like those in our discussion, do understand the necessity for and advantage of testing. They also recognize drawbacks to some types of testing, particularly those with time limits. Further, the students in our portrait believe that tests should accurately measure students' skills. Timed assessments, for example, can make students feel "pressured," to use Alex's word, and unable to do their best work.

But we know that assessment should be a part of our teaching. Why? Because we need it. We use it to measure progress, to decide what instruction is

necessary, to keep us on our toes. We consistently monitor our students' performance through tests: teacher-made tests, end-of-unit tests, weekly spelling tests,
diagnostic tests. Then we sit down and interpret the results. Did most of our students get it? Who needs another go-round? Who needs some prompting to try
harder? To study more? Was our explanation clear enough? Should we go over it
again with the whole class or just a few? Assessment results are guides that help us
plan what to do next. And, we should be tracking our students' ability to read fluently to meet the requirements mandated by the NCLB act.

Ways to Assess Fluency

Valencia and Buly (2004), remind us that "a test score, like a fever, is a symptom
that demands more specific analysis of the problem" (p. 520). If we believe we've
identified a "nonfluent reader," there are a number of different tests we can administer to further the analysis.

We begin by examining the level at which a student is reading on-level materials. Sometimes, we read material easily, with almost 100 percent understanding.
No word difficulty, a familiarity that we can apply to the text to help us understand it, a "walk in the park." We call this is our "independent reading level."
Occasionally, we run across text that is more difficult. Some of the terms are unfamiliar, but we can still make out the meaning. We might skip a word or three, or
reread a sentence, but we get the gist of it. Because we could use a bit of help with
such text, this is our "instructional level." But, if we pick up a textbook on a subject foreign to us, with words and concepts we've never encountered, we are very
likely to stumble over the first paragraph and close the book quickly. This text is
written at our "frustration level." We get little or no meaning from our attempts at
reading it.

The three levels are determined statistically by word accuracy and the degree
of comprehension: independent (99 percent word accuracy and at least 90 percent
understanding), instructional (95 percent word accuracy and at least 75 percent
understanding), and frustration (less than 90 percent word accuracy and understanding at about 50 percent). It's worth remembering that a text's difficulty will
vary depending on the reading level of the student. In other words, a text that's at
the independent level for Alex, from our discussion group above, might very well
be at the frustration level for someone like Felicia, two grades below him. So,
when we ask our students to read fluently, we need to be certain that the text is at
least at their instructional level, if not at their independent level. Otherwise, they
will not be able to perform those skills that constitute fluency, i.e., prosody, automatic word recognition, phrasing, and interpreting punctuation.

CHOOSING THE METHOD

Since a text written at a particular grade level may not be at the instructional level of every student in the class, the number 1 question teachers need to ask if a student is struggling with a text is whether the text is at his frustration level. If so, then we cannot expect the student to be able to read it fluently yet. There is a second question we need to ask as well. Recall how the students in our discussion group agreed that their teachers would remind the student reading orally to "read with expression." That's effective only if the student knows *how* to "read with expression." So we might ask ourselves: "Did I explain clearly what I meant? Did I show my students how to read with expression?"

If we have made sure the student is reading text at his or her instructional level and that he or she understands what we mean by "reading with expression," but the student still reads word by word in a monotone, then that student most likely needs practice in reading fluently.

An experienced teacher can determine whether or not a student is a fluent reader by listening. A fluent reader will read aloud with natural expression, will show very little hesitation in recognizing words, and will phrase correctly. For most of our students, such an informal assessment will suffice. For others, we may need more reliable measures. Jane recently administered an informal reading inventory, or IRI, to her nephew Nate. Most education majors in college learn how to administer such a test in an advanced reading course. The advantage of an IRI is that a teacher can use it to determine students' reading levels. The disadvantage is that it's time-consuming, making it impractical to use as an assessment tool for every student in the class. There are many published informal reading inventories, which come with complete directions for administering them. We've listed several published informal inventories in the bibliography, including the one Jane chose to use: the Critical Reading Inventory. She used this IRI because, in addition to graded selections and comprehension questions, the test also provides a rubric for evaluating fluency.

In Marie Clay's Reading Recovery program, teachers are trained to administer a "running record" of students' oral reading. This is yet another option we can choose for determining a student's instructional level—and whether the student's oral reading is fluent at that level. In this procedure, as described in Burns, Roe & Ross's *Teaching Reading in Today's Elementary Schools* (1992), the student reads a selection at three different levels. The student is familiar with the first selection, having just finished the book. The second is written on a level that is more difficult. The third is easier. As the student reads aloud, the teacher makes a check above every word read correctly. For words read incorrectly or "miscued," the teacher writes a coded mark indicating the type of miscue. After the student has finished, the teacher analyzes the results. What was it that made the student do or say what he or she did? Comparing the three samples, the teacher can determine the student's strengths and weaknesses. A running record provides a quicker and easier way to determine the level at which a student can read fluently. If the student isn't fluent even at the easiest level, we can assume that the student has developed habits that need to be broken.

The National Assessment of Educational Progress (NAEP) test uses an interesting device to measure students' fluency. The selection used to evaluate a student's fluency is one that he or she has read prior to the assessment and has read silently. During the assessment, the student reads the text again, first silently and then aloud. Teachers use a rubric to determine whether the fluency the student demonstrates in the oral reading is acceptable. We have included the NAEP rubric below. It is also available at the NAEP Web site.

NAEP RUBRIC FOR DETERMINING FLUENCY

Level 4 Reads primarily in large, meaningful phrase groups. Although some regressions, repetitions, and deviations from text may be present, these do not appear to detract from the overall structure of the story. Preservation of the author's syntax is consistent; some or most of the story is read with expressive interpretation.

Level 3 Reads primarily in three- or four-word phrase groups. Some small groupings may be present. However, the majority of phrasing seems appropriate and preserves the syntax of the author. Little or no expressive interpretation is present.

Level 2 Reads primarily in two-word phrases with some three- or four-word groupings. Some word-by-word reading may be present. Word-by-word groups may seem awkward and unrelated to target context of sentence or passage.

Level 1 Reads primarily word by word. Occasional two-word phrases may occur, but these are infrequent and/or they do not observe meaningful syntax.

It is fairly simple to determine whether a student reads fluently during oral reading. But it's more difficult with silent reading—and much reading in the middle grades is silent. What, then, can teachers do? We can interview the student to see if, indeed, the same techniques the student applies in oral reading carry over to silent reading. We have devised a short evaluation tool (below) we might use to assess the silent reading fluency of a student whose oral reading is fluent.

QUESTIONS FOR EVALUATING FLUENCY IN SILENT READING

- Can you hear your voice in your head as you read silently—thinking the words as you read with your eyes?

- If the sentence you are reading silently doesn't make sense, what strategy do you use? I'll read these possibilities and you just tell me "yes" or "no" or "sometimes":

Y   N   S   I just keep on reading.

Y   N   S   I go back and reread the sentence to see if I read all the words right.

Y   N   S   I go back and reread and try to understand what the sentence means.

Y   N   S   I check to see if I missed a punctuation mark.

Y   N   S   I wasn't paying attention when I read the sentence. So I reread it to see if it makes sense. If it doesn't, I go back to where I was paying attention, and read the part after that. This time I try to concentrate.

Y   N   S   I ask for help.

Of late, it seems that the most popular way to assess fluency is by measuring a student's per-minute oral reading speed. You will note that we do not include this method as a tool for measuring fluency. That omission was deliberate. Many respected literacy experts (Samuels & Farstrup, 2006) have found fault with such measures. Selections used are usually on "grade" level rather than on the student's independent or instructional reading level. Many of these so-called fluency assessments also fail to tap into comprehension. Students tend to equate "fluency" with speed rather than with those features that experts such as Woods & Moe (1999) have listed in their rubric: reading words in meaningful phrases, using pitch, stress, and intonation to convey meaning, using punctuation to divide the text into units of meaning, and pacing well.

There are two questions we teachers need to ask ourselves when reviewing any fluency assessment results. First, is this consistent performance or is it an aberration? One success is not a victory, nor one slip a failure. Jane remembers one student—a good student, generally—who did poorly when she asked him to read aloud. When she talked with him about his oral reading, she discovered that there had been a disturbance in his home and he hadn't slept at all the night before the test. How could he perform well, upset as he was and without rest?

And second, who or what is to blame for these test results? Are we doing our best to encourage fluency? Do we ask our students to read text too difficult for them? Do we practice the outmoded round-robin reading? Do our students recognize the importance of reading fluently? Do we present a model of good oral reading for our students to imitate?

WHERE DO WE GO FROM HERE?

Once we have identified nonfluent readers, where do we go from here? Whether we have used one of the many assessments of fluency or our own best judgment, the next step is to decide how we can best help these students become better readers. So, let's look at one of the many rubrics available for assessing fluency and go from there. Using the criteria established by Woods & Moe for identifying fluency, listed above, we analyze Nate's reading from the IRI Jane administered, which reflects many of the same difficulties Nate experienced in the lessons on reading sentences fluently (page 26), and chunking words to phrase properly (page 83). Having identified the areas of concern, we make some recommendations for improvement.

Reading words in meaningful phrases

Nate attempts to do this but is hindered because of his word-recognition skills. He relies too much on phonics rather than committing the whole word to memory. We would devise ways to build up his sight vocabulary. Games based on well-known favorites—such as Parcheesi, Concentration, or bingo—hold the attention of students like Nate. We would design games using words and phrases wherever they might fit, as we did in Read-O. To win the point, Nate would have to read the phrase smoothly. Once he accomplished that, we would move to short sentences. We would also create flash cards, with the word on one side and the word in a phrase on the other side. If he was able to read both sides without hesitation, Nate would get a check. Three checks and that card would go into the "I know it" pile.

Using pitch stress and intonation to convey meaning

Imitation works well with this. Practicing the same sentence with different punctuation (I did it! I did it? *I* did it.) helps. Activities such as telling jokes or Readers Theater also help students use pitch, stress, and intonation. Nate rose to the occasion when we prepared the comedy show for the family. His first reading was hesitant, lacking the needed pitch, stress, and intonation. However, after practicing several times, he was able to carry off an excellent performance. Motivation plays a very important part in learning.

Using punctuation to divide the text into units of meaning

Sometimes students are so intent on the words that they overlook punctuation. Marking punctuation with a highlighter can help, as can having students practice reading longer sentences, pausing, and phrasing appropriately. Nate needs a few starts before he gets into a longer sentence. It isn't easy to read a script cold the first time. Encourage students to look it over and get a sense of the meaning before reading it aloud. We should avoid asking a student to read a piece aloud before having read it silently. The round-robin reading strategy that many of us experienced as students should not be used regularly in the classroom. It reinforces many poor habits that affect fluency.

Pacing well

Nate's hesitation on words affects his pacing considerably. Because we were in a "testing" mode, I needed to follow the protocol, which required him to read at his frustration level. It was impossible for him to keep up his pace because of the many words he stumbled on. So, first and foremost, we must use the appropriate texts, preferably at the independent level, when asking students to pace their oral reading. We can model reading a sentence for them and have them imitate us by reading it back to us. Allowing students to read the text silently first will help them with their pacing.

FINAL COMMENTS

I reminded Nate that whether he was reading silently or orally, he should be practicing the same strategies. I told him to listen to "the voice in his head." He should hear the same things that he hears when he reads aloud as he hears in his head. He should also be monitoring his reading. If something doesn't make sense, he needs to go back. Reread. Maybe he misread a word. Maybe he missed a punctuation mark. Whatever it is, the reading he does has to make sense. Nate is actually good at that—maybe too good. He often repeats phrases that don't make sense until he discovers his mistake. I viewed that characteristic as a plus and pointed out that the more words he recognizes on sight, the fewer times he will have to do that.

Learning from Nate, then, what is the bottom line for improving fluency with students? We have listed several important considerations:

• Use text written at the students' independent level.
• Model the right way for them.
• Focus on one skill at a time.
• Allow students to build gradually on the skills they have mastered.
• Provide practice that motivates them.

Throughout this book, our lessons address these considerations in various ways. We encourage you to use our lessons and craft additional lessons and strategies that support and build fluency.

EPILOGUE

Taking Fluency to the Highest Level With Choral Speaking

Before this book was even a proposal, we knew that the Gloucester County Christian School Choral Speaking Group must have a part. When we listen to their reading performances, we hear fluency at its highest level. Beautiful, expressive, and lyrical, their choral speaking epitomizes what we understand to be fluency.

Under the direction of Janet Iles, a friend and colleague, this 15-member group of juniors and seniors has won the New Jersey state title seven years running and places in the top three at national-level competitions. In March 2007, at Bob Jones University in Greenville, South Carolina, they walked away with the national title!

In what we call choral speaking, diction, inflection, and timing are equally critical as are facial expressions and hand and head motions. Group members practice for an hour twice a week beginning in November. As director, Janet researches scripts, often rewriting them. This year she used a different approach and selected the entire text of a Dr. Seuss book, *Horton Hatches the Egg*, adapting it to individual and group voices. In initial practices, group members read from scripts, practicing until synchrony is achieved. Students listen to one another to make sure they're going at the same pace. In this sense, the group's work is much like the choral reading practice described in Chapter 4.

Eventually, group members memorize the script, and the choral reading moves to choral speaking. We close our book with a concluding portrait of the 2007 award-winning performance of this most talented and disciplined group of students. But we suggest, too, that any group of students can plan, practice, and present choral readings or choral-speaking performances.

PORTRAIT: HORTON HATCHES THE EGG

Heads high, shoulders back, they march in single file. Girls dressed in soft green dresses, boys in shirts of the same color and black trousers. Poise and confidence show in their eyes and demeanor as they assume their places on the stage risers. Ready, eyes on their director, they await the signal. The audience quiets in expectation.

"Hello," says the first speaker. "Gloucester County Christian School presents Dr. Seuss's poem *Horton Hatches the Egg*." The entire group chimes in on the word *Horton*; in precise synchrony they drop their heads and pause. With different speakers taking different roles, the poem-story of Horton the elephant's adventures caring for Mayzie bird's egg unfolds, with solo voices alternating with all voices in unison. The characters come to life through simple, well-timed gestures and lines of dialogue. At one point, hunters arrive and carry off Horton, his egg, and the tree across the ocean to Miami, Florida. Here the performers crescendo, voices rising and falling, mimicking the rolling ocean.

Boys: A horrible trip, a horrible trip

Girls: Rolling, rolling, rolling

Horton: I'm gonna be seasick

All: He's gonna be seasick

All: Yu-uck, yu-uck, yu-uck! (*All bend over holding stomachs and pretend to be seasick.*)

The final verses are recited in unison. The last line, "They sent him home happy, one hundred percent," sets off a round of applause and cheers. The group bows and quietly leaves the stage. But a glimmer of a smile on each face shows. They know it. A job well done! The competition ends and they wait in anxious expectation. Finally, the judges announce . . . Gloucester County Christian School. National winners!

Fluency. Expression, automaticity, correct phrasing—we listen for these components in the voices of our students as they read aloud. And we certainly hear them in the Gloucester County Christian School's winning performance. Engagement, motivation, and the promise of an audience fuel the will to practice and to be *good*! We end by inviting all of you to not only teach fluency but to demand it of your readers. Know your students and create inviting lessons. Find texts or use original writing to perform choral-reading and choral speaking performances of your own. Use our lessons to help you begin. We wish you happy hunting and many successful fluency performances.

Bibliography

PROFESSIONAL RESOURCES CITED

Allen, J. (1999). *Words, words, words: Teaching vocabulary in grades 4–12*. York, Maine: Stenhouse.

Allington, R. & Cunningham, P. (1983). Fluency, the neglected goal. *The Reading Teacher, 36.* 556-561.

Applegate, M., Quinn, K. & Applegate, A. (2004). *The critical reading inventory.* Upper Saddle River, NJ: Pearson/Merrill/Prentice Hall.

Beck, I. & McKeown, M. (1991). Conditions of vocabulary acquisition. In P. D. Pearson (Ed.), *The handbook of reading research* (Vol. 2, pp. 789–814). New York: Longman.

Beck, I., McKeown, M. & Kucan, L.(2002). *Bringing Words to Life: Robust Vocabulary Instruction.* New York: The Guilford Press.

Blachowicz, C. & Fisher, P. (2002). *Teaching vocabulary in all classrooms* (2nd Ed.).

New York: Prentice Hall.

Burns, P., Roe, B. & Ross, E. (1992). *Teaching reading in today's elementary schools* (5th Ed.). Boston: Houghton Mifflin.

Calfee, R. C. & Drum, P. A. (1986). Research on teaching reading. In M.C. Wittrock (Ed.) *Handbook on Research on Teaching* (3rd Ed. pp. 804–849). New York: Macmillan.

Cole, A. (1998). Scaffolding beginning readers: Micro and macro cues teachers use during student oral reading. *The Reading Teacher. 50*(5). 450–461.

Cassidy, J. & Cassidy, D. (2006). What's hot, what's not for 2006. *Reading Today, 23* (3), 1.

Dowhower, S. L. (1987). Effects of repeated reading on second grade transitional readers' fluency and comprehension. *Reading Research Quarterly. 22,* 389–486.

Flynt, E. S. & Cooter, R. Jr. (2001). *Reading inventory for the classroom.* Upper Saddle River, NJ: Merrill/Prentice Hall.

Graves, D. (1983). *Writing: Teachers and children at work.* Portsmouth, NH: Heinemann.

Griffith, L. & Rasinski, T. (2004). A focus on fluency: How one teacher incorporated fluency with her reading curriculum. *The Reading Teacher. 58*(2). 126–137.

Hale, C. (1999). *Sin and syntax: How to craft wickedly effective prose.* New York: Broadway Books.

Heard, G. (1995). *Writing toward home.* Portsmouth, NH: Heinemann.

Hudson, R., Lane, H. & Pullen, P. (2005). Reading fluency assessment and instruction: what, why, and how? *The Reading Teacher, 58*(8), 702–714.

Lubliner, S. (2004). Help for struggling upper-grade elementary readers. *The Reading Teacher. 57*(5). 430–438.

Johnson, D. (2001). *Vocabulary in the elementary and middle school.* Boston: Allyn and Bacon.

Kouider, M. & Thompson, H. (2006). How problems of reading fluency and comprehension are related to difficulties in syntactic awareness skills among fifth graders. *Reading Research and Instruction Journal, 46,* 1, 73–94.

Kuhn, M. & Stahl, S. (2000). *Fluency: A review of developmental and remedial practices.* Ann Arbor, MI: Center for the Improvement of Early Reading Achievement.

McKeown, M., Beck, I., Omanson, R. & Pople, M. (1985, Autumn). Some effects of the nature and frequency of vocabulary instruction on the knowledge and use of words. *Reading Research Quarterly, 20,* 522–535.

Opitz, M. & Rasinski, T. (1998). *Good-bye round robin: 25 effective oral reading strategies.* Portsmouth: Heinemann.

O'Shea, L. Sindelar, P. & O'Shea, D. (1985). The effects of repeated readings and attentional cues on reading fluency and comprehension. *Journal of Reading Behavior,* 17, 19–142.

Pikulski, J. (2006). Fluency: A developmental and language perception in S. J. Samuels & A. Farstrup, (Eds.), *What research has to say about fluency instruction* (pp. 70-80). Newark, DE: International Reading Association.

Pikulski, J. & Chard, D. (2005). Fluency: Bridge between decoding and reading comprehension. *The Reading Teacher, 58*(6), 510.

Rasinski, T. (2003). *The fluent reader.* New York: Scholastic Professional Books.

Samuels, S. & Farstrup, A. (2006). *What research has to say about fluency instruction,* Newark, DE: International Reading Association.

Schreiber, P. (1980). On the acquisition of reading fluency. *Journal of Reading Behavior, 12,* 177–186.

Stahl, S., Heubach, K. & Cramond, B. (1997). *Fluency-oriented instruction.* Athens, GA: National Reading Research Center, University of Georgia.

Terban, M. (1993). *Checking your grammar and getting it right.* New York: Scholastic.

Valencia, S. & Buly, M. (2004). Behind test scores: What struggling readers really need. *The Reading Teacher. 57*(6). 520–533.

Weaver, C. (1998). *Lessons to share: On teaching grammar in context.* Portsmouth, NH: Boyton/Cook/Heinemann.

Weaver, C. (1996). *Teaching grammar in context.* Portsmouth, NH: Boyton/Cook/Heinemann.

Woods, M. & Moe, A. (1999). *Analytical reading inventory* (6th Ed.). Upper Saddle River, NJ: Merrill/Prentice Hall.

CHILDREN'S LITERATURE CITED

Avi. (2002). *Crispin: The cross of the lead.* New York: Hyperion.

Brown, Margaret Wise. (1942). *Runaway bunny.* New York and London, Harper.

Creech, Sharon. (1998). *Bloomability.* New York: HarperCollins Publishers.

Creech, Sharon. (2005). *Replay.* New York: Joanna Cotler Books.

Evangelista, Beth. (2005). *Gifted.* New York: Walker & Co.

Fleischman, Paul. (1988). *Joyful noise: Poems for two voices.* New York: Harper & Rowe.

Hesse, Karen. (1997). *Out of the dust.* New York: Scholastic.

Hoose, Philip & Hannah. (1998). *Hey, little ant.* Berkeley, CA: Tricycle Press.

Lowry, Lois. (1989). *Number the stars.* Boston: Houghton Mifflin.

Marshall, James. (1977). *Miss Nelson is missing.* Boston: Houghton Mifflin.

Spinelli, Jerry. (1990). *Maniac Magee.* Boston: Little, Brown.

Sullivan, J. (2003). The aurora borealis. *Hopscotch for Girls, 15*(2) 34–35.

Weitzman, Ilana, Blank, Eva, Green, Rosanne, and Wright, Mike. (2000). *Jokelopedia: The biggest, silliest, dumbest joke book ever!* New York: Workman.

Index